15

Minutes

One Suspect Dead
Two Cops Indicted
Three Families Changed Forever

R. Blaine Jorg

To my Lord and Savior Jesus Christ, who has given me far more than
I deserve in my life.

Discretion will protect you,
And understanding will guard you.
Wisdom will save you from the ways of the wicked men,
From men whose words are perverse,
Who leave the straight paths
To walk in dark ways,
Who delight in doing wrong
And rejoice in the perverseness of evil,
Whose paths are crooked And who are devious in their ways.

PROVERBS 2: 11-15

"That the Commonwealth may have a
Government of Laws and not of men"

Inscribed on the north side of the Hamilton County Court House

Table of Contents

In the last moments of his life, while in hand cuffs, Roger Owensby Jr. had to be scared to death when he looked into the eyes of his killer...Robert Blaine Jorg.

Don't let Blaine Jorg get away with Murder

END Racial Profiling & Police Brutality

PRISON FOR OFFICER PATRICK CATON FOR THE BRUTAL MURDER OF ROGER OWENSBY.

Introduction

During the last Century, the American society underwent enormous change, as the country evolved from an agriculture-based economy to one centered on the production of goods and services.

Two of the greatest challenges to America during that time were the Great Depression of the 1930's, in which millions of citizens were unable to secure gainful employment, and the civil rights movement of the 1960s, in which Americans of all races demanded social justice for all.

The United States Congress responded to both crises by enacting legislation designed to alleviate and remedy these national emergencies. While such legislation accorded much of the desired results, such Federal laws would have unforeseen and undesired consequences with the progression of time.

In 1935 Congress passed the National Labor Relations Act, which facilitated workers in the forming of labor unions. Millions of working people nationwide formed such unions during that time, with improved wages and working conditions one result.

Unfortunately, members of organized crime were quick to seize upon the opportunities for corruption that the emergence of a national labor union presented. While the televised hearings of U.S. Senator Estes Kefauver's committee after World War II and the treatment of the growing crisis by such Hollywood films as On the Waterfront served a vital purpose in altering the average American to this new crime wave, such events inadvertently created and perpetuated a myth, that many Italian-Americans are involved in "The Mafia", or organized crime.

The fact is that a very small percentage of Italian-Americans are involved in criminal activity, and that same fact applies to all ethnic groups in the United States, including recent immigrants to this country, as well as to the men and women of America's law enforcement community.

After the assassination of President Kennedy in 1963, Congress acted to secure Kennedy's legacy by passing the Civil Rights Act of 1964. The intent of this law was to enact Federal protection to minority citizens by providing substantial penalties to those in law enforcement who unlawfully violated a citizen's civil rights.

Within two decades, however, unforeseen consequences would emerge, as criminals, most often drug dealers, and their corrupt lawyers perverted such legislation in order to lodge fabricated charges of civil rights violations against members of America's law enforcement community. Publicity seeking, self-appointed "community activist", as well as politicians, would also seize upon this tactic in order to pursue their own selfish agenda, empowering the very criminals that preyed upon the communities they supposedly represented.

Congress has been slow to respond to both these national challenges to law enforcement. Two decades after the Kefauver Hearings, Congress passed the Racketeer Influenced and Corrupt Organizations Act of 1970, (RICO), which armed Federal Prosecutors with new laws aimed at organized crime and their control over labor unions. These statutes, however would languish another 15 years before being utilized by a Federal Prosecutor in New York, Rudolph Giuliani.

In regards to the growing incidences of criminals invoking civil rights legislation to falsely accuse members of law enforcement of crimes, Congress has, once again, been slow to act. While hearings on this growing crisis have been heard by various committees in recent years, no legislation has been enacted. The great irony here is that the civil rights of members of America's law enforcement community are being violated by the perversion of existing civil rights statutes.

The story you are about to read is that of a dedicated police officer who, in 13 minutes of his career, had his life turned upside-down. On the night of November 7, 2000 Cincinnati police officer R. Blaine Jorg left home, said goodbye to his wife ready to sacrifice his life, if necessary to save the citizens of his city from the scourge of drug dealers. The events of that night would see Jorg branded a racist and murderer, in a nightmare that would take away years of Jorg's life.

In a sad commentary on our times, Officer Jorg is not alone. Across America, the brave men and women of our law enforcement community are engaged in a war, an undeclared "war on drugs" in which various members of the United States government are on the wrong side of the law. Some of these men and women on the front lines of this war are killed in the line of duty, some have their careers put on hold by false accusations, and some even go to prison for crimes they did not commit.

This is the story of a country at war, facing an enemy within.

Joe Occhipinti
Executive Director
National Police Defense Foundation

Prologue

When I went to work on the afternoon of November 7, 2000, I didn't think my life would be turned upside-down. I was a Cincinnati police officer with five-and-a-half years of experience under my belt. My partner, Pat Caton, and I were assigned to District Four, beat five, Roselawn and Bond Hill. We had patrolled this area of the city together for three-and-a-half years. We had no idea that we were headed for a tragic nightmare that to this day still affects us.

On this night we were going to have a confrontation with a suspected drug dealer who allegedly assaulted another police officer about six weeks prior. Unfortunately, this meeting would end up with the death of that suspect, Roger Owensby Jr., a death that would only inflame the already unstable atmosphere of the city of Cincinnati. Sixteen hours later, a subject by the name of Jeffery Irons would be involved in a confrontation with police in a neighboring district, where he would be shot and killed.

I've replayed that night in my mind every day since November 7; there isn't one thing I would change. My partner, Pat, and I were tried and convicted in the press, then our case was brought in front of a grand jury. Pat was indicted on assault, and I was indicted for involuntary manslaughter and assault. Even though both of us were found not guilty, this event has had damning results to each officer involved, to the family of Roger Owensby Jr., and to the city of Cincinnati.

The whole case spiraled out of control to the point where it seemed to take on a life of its own. Then, in April of 2001, another horrible incident took place in Cincinnati. Police Officer Stephen Roach shot and killed a suspect, Timothy Thomas. Cries for justice rang out through the city. Unsatisfied with the city's response, the streets erupted with riots. For a week, the city was at war with itself. Public officials called for order, but it seemed as though no one was listening. After the criminal trials, the justice department came in and investigated the police department. My integrity and values were questioned. I lost the one thing I never thought I would lose, my faith. My life went to the ruins of the deepest part of hell.

It seemed as though my partner and I were being put on trial for all of the past actions of Cincinnati police officers. Between 1995 and November

7, 2000, there were 11 people killed by the members of Cincinnati Police Department. Even though all the past situations were investigated and the officers cleared of any wrongdoing, I can't help but feel that Pat and I were paying for their perceived sins. I reached the point where I knew my career was over in Cincinnati, so I moved on to another police department, just out-side of Cincinnati, Pierce Township. Even though it was a great move, life didn't get any easier. I used to have a solid faith, but now I had developed a great hatred for God. I became suicidal, and extremely dangerous. Then, I retired from Pierce Township with post traumatic stress disorder. I sunk even lower into a black hole. I may have been alive, but I wasn't living.

Thirteen minutes. That's all it took for my life to change. That's the amount of time it took for Pat and I to stop Roger Owensby, place him into custody and then find him unresponsive in the back seat of a police car.

I wonder why this case is still making news, still being talked about. I think it is because no one has ever heard my side. Well I can tell you this: when this part of my life is over, I never want to talk about it again.

At the criminal investigation section on the night of the incident, none of the officers involved made a statement. Each of us was told by our FOP attorney to take the fifth. I did make a statement to the police department's internal investigation section, and at my deposition for the Owensby's civil suit. But only bits and pieces of those statements were ever made public. From day one I was hushed by one attorney after another. Now the civil suits are all decided. Now all the charges are gone. Now I can tell my story.

My wife and I moved to the country in effort to get out of the spotlight. It didn't help. Even in the middle of nowhere, I was recognized by people. I tried to get part-time jobs to get me out of the house and do something constructive. It didn't work. At one job, one of the employees found out who I was and gave me the nick name "nigger slayer." I quit the next day. I continue to go through counseling, medication changes and therapy. Even with the help they bring, they still don't take away the flashbacks and the depression. I will be dealing with this the rest of my life.

My farm is my safety zone; I don't leave home unless I absolutely have to. My circle of friends has become very small. There are few people I will let into my circle. My entire trust factor was tainted the night that Roger Owensby died. My trust weakened both in man and in the law.

I see Roger Owensby a lot. He's in my nightmares. There are many times I have woken up in the middle of the night because of dreams that are terrifyingly real. Every day and night I toil with what happened on the night of November 7. I try not to think about it, but it is a part of me now.

This book is a part of my therapy. I can see the healing that is coming with it. This book gives me the opportunity to finally tell people my story and to make all the facts available. I would like to thank all the officers, fire personnel and community members for all the support they have shown the officers involved in this case.

Forward

Cincinnati was a wonderful place to live. I grew up north of Cincinnati in a place called Twenty Mile Stand. In the '50s and '60s, it was truly farm country. I remember that I was so excited when I enrolled at the University of Cincinnati and was able to move near the campus in the city. The city was fun and vibrant. After college and as my interests developed, I enjoyed the Art Museum, the Symphony, even opera. We had season tickets to the ballet. We had season passes to the Zoo. My wife and I enjoyed going downtown, having dinner and going to Playhouse in the Park. We had professional sports, the Reds and the Bengals. Cincinnati was a wonderful and exciting place to live.

We always felt safe. People were friendly and kind. Folks smiled at you, for no apparent reason. Cincinnati was the kind of place we wanted to raise our family.

I cared about those kinds of things: the people, the cultural advantages. When I graduated from law school, I had the chance to work in the city government. I got a job in the City of Cincinnati Prosecutor's Office in 1978. I went to work in city government not because I couldn't get a job somewhere else. I chose to work in city government because I cared. I felt I could make a difference. Cincinnati was a place where I could devote my professional talents. It was my home.

As time passed through the '80s, I rose in the ranks of the city. In 1981, I moved to the civil side of the Solicitor's Office, the office of the city attorney. I became a senior assistant, Chief Trial Counsel and eventually Deputy Solicitor. During those years, I learned about politics. As I saw decisions made at the higher levels of government, I learned that decisions are not always made with an eye toward the interests of the public. Politics is a dirty business. I learned that sometimes politics trumped good judgment

In 1992, I became the Safety Director for the city. Cincinnati utilizes a city manager form of government. There is a city council to set policy, and a city manager to run the day-to-day operations of city government. A number of departments exist in the city, like Public Works, Parks, Recreation, Purchasing, etc. One of those departments was the Safety Department. The Safety Department included the Police Division and the Fire Division. I was the director of the Safety Department, and the administrative head of the Cincinnati Police Chief.

As Safety Director, I learned a whole new kind of politics: racial politics. Racial issues have always existed in Cincinnati, just like they do in every city. Cincinnati politicians and African-American leaders learned that race is a potent weapon to use for political advantage. Cincinnati was about to change.

I left city government at the end of 1995. I spent 17 years as a public servant. I'm very proud of my government service. I'll never do it again.

After I left the city workforce, I went into private practice. My law office was in downtown Cincinnati. I had a private law office in downtown Cincinnati since 1978, when I became a lawyer. I began to notice changes, big changes after I left city employment. African-American leaders began to complain about black men being killed by police. It seemed to make no difference to these so-called leaders that some of the African-American men were shooting police officers or otherwise trying to kill the police officers when they were shot by the police. Blaine talks about these African-American men killed in encounters with police in this book. You judge for yourself whether there was cause for alarm among the decent, hard-working folks in the African-American community. To these leaders, one African-American man killed by police was one too many, regardless of his misconduct at the time of his death.

In November 2000, the incident between Roger Owensby, Jr., and Police Officers Blaine Jorg and Pat Caton occurred. With the Owensby incident, Cincinnati began to change. Without investigating the facts, politicians began to pontificate. The politicians decided to let Jorg and Caton "twist in the wind." It was simpler to blame Jorg and Caton than to deal with the racial backlash of the truth. So Jorg and Caton were abandoned by their employer, abandoned by city council, abandoned by their own department and were indicted. In April 2001, the incident between Timothy Thomas and Police Officer Stephen Roach occurred. After the April 2001 incident, the "Cincinnati riots," happened. Roach was also indicted. Jorg, Caton and Roach were all found not guilty. But, no politician seemed to care about the facts, as long as the African-American community didn't blame or implicate them in the blame for the death of another African-American man. This was racial politics at its best, or worst, depending on your perspective.

I didn't represent Jorg or Caton, or Roach, in the criminal proceedings. I'm a civil lawyer. But, I represented Blaine Jorg in a civil lawsuit trying to hold the Coroner and city leaders responsible for making Jorg a scapegoat. I've been doing those types of government cases for over 25 years. I told Blaine that the "civil rights" laws were not created to help an injured party like him, but were designed to protect the government from suit. And we were unsuccessful. The judge would not let us investigate through the discovery process and dismissed the suit before we could take even one deposition. I represented Roach after he left the Cincinnati Police Department to try to escape the unwarranted political attacks on him. When the Cincinnati Police Internal Investigation Report was published, months after Roach left the Cincinnati Police, his new employer suspended him from further police work. I represented Roach and got his job back and got him back out on the street helping the citizens of a suburban police department. When the city of Cincinnati fired Caton claiming that he beat a hand-cuffed Owensby, I represented Caton. That case went to arbitration before a neutral arbitrator under the provisions of the union contract. The neutral arbitrator found that Caton had not hit a hand-cuffed Owensby. Funny isn't it, when a neutral person, not controlled by the politics of Cincinnati or the media, examined the evidence, there was no case against Caton. Caton got his job back and it will cost the city hundreds of thousands of dollars in back pay and benefits for letting politics control their policing decisions. Too bad Blaine didn't have that same opportunity to have a neutral arbitrator or a court hear his side of the story.

But, this book is Blaine's opportunity. It is the first time he can tell you, the public, what really happened. Not the media hype, not the politically correct version; the real version. The same story he had told from the beginning but nobody in politics in Cincinnati, nobody in the media wanted to hear. Why? Because then they would have to admit that what was done to Blaine was a travesty. Politicians and media types don't like to make mistakes. Forget about the truth, where is the next vote coming from, what is tomorrow's headline.

So what has happened in Cincinnati since the politicians decided that votes were more important than the truth? Since politicians decided that Jorg was expendable? Cincinnati, my Cincinnati, has forever changed. After the "riots," African-American leaders (the actual number of "leaders" and their followers could be counted on your hands and toes) called for a boycott of Cincinnati. African-American leaders called for amnesty for rioters as a prerequisite to eliminating the boycott. Their message was clear: violence and riots were acceptable, and we support your misconduct and will fight to make sure you are not held accountable for your misconduct. With that message, a huge change occurred in Cincinnati. Cincinnati is again on-track to record the largest number of homicides in history. Every morning the news is filled with shootings, deaths, crime, crime, crime. The Maisonette, a Mobile Five Star restaurant in downtown Cincinnati for forty years, had to close its doors. Why? It is easier to stay in the suburbs: it's difficult to eat when you have to keep dodging bullets in downtown.

I'm no social scientist, but the message in Cincinnati is clear. When the politicians don't support the police, crime will skyrocket. Disrespect for police leads to lawlessness. When crime escalates, decent, hard-working people leave in droves. City leaders can't understand why people are moving out of Cincinnati in record numbers. They really don't want to understand. Because if they understand, they have to accept that the fault lies with them, and the criminals that they have empowered in Cincinnati.

So, I've learned important lessons over the years. I've learned that I really couldn't make all that much of a difference after all. I believe that for folks to succeed in society, they have to go to school, they have to get a job, and they have to work. If you have job and have to get up to go to work, you won't be standing on a street corner at 3 a.m. and end up another homicide statistic. And I've learned that supporting your police is the most important single step that any person can take to have a safer community. Examine the conduct of police officers, but don't blame police officers who while doing their job end up dealing with thugs who want to run, fight, shoot or otherwise cause serious harm to the men and women who risk their lives to make us safe.

For myself, I've solved the problem. Last year I moved to the country. Two months ago I moved my law office to the country. Cincinnati is not the place I want to raise my family. Cincinnati is not the place I want to run my business. I couldn't be happier. I couldn't feel safer. How sad.

William Gustavson
September 2006

Chapter 1

13 Minutes

On November 7, 2000, my partner, Pat Caton, and I started our shift at 1 pm as usual. Later in the evening I worked with a group of kids ages of 15-20. They were police explorers and I was one of their advisors. At about 7:30, Pat and I left for a dinner break at Empress Chili. We never got there.

Officers Alex Hasse and Darren Sellers had stopped a subject at Sam's Carry Out and found some marijuana on him. Apparently, the officers had run out of pay-out tickets, so they communicated on their in-car computer: "If there was anyone close, could they bring us a form?" Well, it was our beat also, so Pat and I went.

The Bond Hill area is well known. It is synonymous with illegal drug activity. You can't swing a dead cat without hitting a drug dealer. This area of Bond Hill consisted of the Huntington Meadows housing project (which has since been closed), Seymour Avenue, Langdon Farm Road, Rhode Island Avenue by Sam's Carry Out, and Bond Hill park. Not a good neighborhood. The very place that city council woman Alicia Reese had requested a directed patrol for drug trafficking. This means a complaint is filed with the police department, and a specific unit or beat officer is assigned to that specific location. Pat and I worked this beat, so we were told by our Sergeant to target all criminal activity in this area. For reasons unknown to me, Ms. Reese denied making this request later while she was a guest on the Bill Cunningham radio show.

We pulled up behind the cruiser, which was parked on the west end of Sam's parking lot. Pat gave a ticket book to Officer Hasse. Pat's talking with Officer Hasse, who is seated in the driver's seat of the vehicle, and I am talking to officer Sellers by the front of the cruiser. Officer Hunter pulls in next to the cruisers. Hunter expresses interest in talking to the prisoner sitting in the back seat of the patrol car. He wanted to know if the prisoner was familiar with a guy known as L.A., who assaulted him during a drug investigation a few weeks earlier.

Sure enough, the prisoner knows L.A but doesn't want to say much else about it. He only tells us that L.A. is a dangerous guy and a local drug dealer.

1

The prisoner said he could ID L.A., but he is also afraid that if L.A. found out who pointed him out, L.A. might come back on him. A moment later, Hunter tells the officers that he has just seen L.A. walking down the other side of the street. Hunter points to an African American man walking away from us. This man crosses the street and goes into a Sunoco station.

"That's the guy who assaulted me," Hunter says.

Hunter grabs Pat by the arm, and says, "Come here with me." Then the two of them climb over the guardrail and start walking toward the store. For a second I'm surprised, because Hunter and Pat aren't exactly bosom buddies. Pat and I had suspicions at the time about Hunter. There was nothing that we could pin point; I guess it was more of a combination of factors. I hustle over and catch up with them.

I meet up with them at the side of the store. Caton tells Hunter to look through the window. Now that the suspect is standing under the lights of the store, and Hunter is much closer, it should be easy to determine if this is the guy who assaulted Hunter. After looking through the window Hunter tells us that he is 90 percent sure that he is the guy. I'm watching and listening, wishing that Hunter was 100 percent sure. Still the next step is obvious: We have to find out.

Pat and I use what is called contact cover. With two officers, one will do all the talking and the other will watch his partner's back. Pat is usually the contact officer, but it's not a hard-fast rule. We will go back and forth depending on the situation. I had it in my gut that the suspect was going to run. I knew he would break through Hunter. Maybe he would get past Pat, but he wasn't going to get past me. I walk from the side of the store to the front. I holster my PR24 (night stick) and stand at the doorway waiting for the suspect to exit. Since Hunter was only 90 percent sure that this was the guy, Pat and I had some doubts whether or not this was the suspect who actually committed the assault on Hunter. We both agreed that we would talk to this gentleman and we would find out that Hunter was mistaken, and we would probably be sending him on his way. If Hunter was 100 percent sure we would have prepared to take him down at gun point without any hesitation.

In front of the store I initiate contact with the suspect. He had just bought an energy drink and two cigars and he was heading toward me. I don't know him. I have never seen him before.

2

"Excuse me sir, could you set your drink down?" I ask him. He sets his drink down and I ask, "Do you have anything on you we need to know about?"

"No." He replied.

Pat joins me on my left side, as I ask, "Do you have any weapons on you?"

"No." He hesitates for a split second, then lifts up his shirt to expose his waist area to show he doesn't have a gun there. He is cooperating and seems to be at ease with us.

"For your safety and mine, do you mind if I pat you down?" I ask.

Again he complies. While I pat him down, I find that he doesn't have any weapons on him. But he has something in his right front pocket, and I have a pretty good idea what it is. Based on my training and experience, I conclude that it is marijuana. At this point in the investigation I couldn't care less, because this is possibly the guy who assaulted a police officer, which is a felony. The possession of marijuana is only a minor misdemeanor. It's not my main focus right now. Besides, I have no legal right to go into his pocket. Not yet, anyway.

Well, we go round and round. What's your name, where do you live, what are you doing here tonight. As soon as he answers one question I ask another, all the while studying his body language and his face.

"When was the last time you ran from the cops?" I asked, it seemed to be a reasonable question.

"I never ran from the cops." He responded.

"Oh, come on, everyone has run now and then, when was the last time you ran from the cops?"

He says nothing.

While I am questioning the suspect, Pat is on my left, and Hunter is standing in the background. Hunter had been working under cover and didn't want to get ID'd just yet. But at this point Hunter steps in and says, "that's him", points at him and again, "that's him." The look on the suspect's face changes and he seems to go rigid for a split second. It's a small thing, but

I don't need to hear anymore. He's going to jail. I grab his left hand and bring it behind his back as I reach for my handcuffs. When he hears the VELCRO on my cuff case he breaks loose and runs. He shoves Hunter and runs past Pat.

Hunter was shoved back pretty far. I run between him and Pat and I catch up to the suspect in about 15 steps. From behind I grab him around the waist and we slam into a parked car. His head and upper body hit the rear of the car, near the tire. We bounce off and stumble backwards. My momentum carries me to the ground, the suspect lands on top of me. This is a bad position for a cop to be in. I immediately try to get out from under him. I see Pat running, yelling into his radio, "4252, 4252. Sunoco lot! We need assistance!" With great effort, I heave against him and the ground. I am able to roll over. Now I have the advantage. The suspect is on his stomach. Unfortunately, my left arm is pinned between him and the pavement.

I struggle to release my arm and begin to understand the strength of the man I'm trying to arrest. He's strong, and fighting me. He tries to roll out from under me. I feel strain on my left elbow and I'm afraid I'm going to hyperextend it. With all my effort, I finally pull my arm free and grab onto his bicep. Now, I have both hands free.

I pull on the suspect's arm, I need to cuff him. Caton secures his legs, and not a minute too soon. The man on the ground may be shorter, and at least 30 pounds lighter than me, but he's powerful and he's fighting mad. In fact, he's stronger than me, which is why I can't get his arm out no matter how hard I try. The suspect is sweating and swearing and fighting like crazy to free himself, but Pat's on the suspect's legs working to get his right arm out. He isn't going anywhere. But he's not going to let us cuff him, either. One of the hardest things to do as a police officer involved in a violent altercation is to cuff someone who has no desire to cooperate.

The suspect begins banging his head against the ground, using it as a lever, a fulcrum, to keep his arm underneath so he can't be handcuffed. I realize that the only way I'm going to get his wrist is to make him unable to use his strength. Two pops to a nerve and the hand should come free. However, getting at the wrist isn't my only concern; I'm also worried that he'll injure himself by hitting his head on the pavement. From the kneeling position I was in, I slide to the ground. I lie next to the suspect and reach in between the ground and his head and slide my arm between the gravel infested blacktop and the suspect's head. His forehead is now cradled in the crook of my arm. It does the trick. His head is immobilized. Then, I bring my right hand over and aim my thumb at a pressure point at the base of his jaw. "Give me your hands! Quit resisting! Give me your hands!" I yell, but he only struggles harder. So I deliver a blow to the pressure point, like I was taught in the academy. Deliver pain to a pressure point and you'll be able to manipulate just about any part of the body. At least that's how it is supposed to work. It takes three blows to this pressure point before his hand begins to come out from under his body.

I don't see the hand but I can feel it. In the darkness and confusion, Pat doesn't see the left arm move either. He only knows that the suspect we are wrestling is incredibly strong. Pat delivers three to five palm strikes to areas on the suspect's arm, stunning nerve endings. I turn to grab the left hand, Pat says to Hunter, who is just standing there, "Mace him, mace him..." When I thought about this later, it made me wonder even more about Hunter, a sworn police officer standing there doing nothing while his fellow officers struggled with this suspect who they were obviously having difficulty placing into handcuffs.

At that point I saw Officers Hodge, Lawson and Sellers arrive on scene. I start bringing my arm out from under Owensby's forehead as Hunter sprays the suspect's face with mace. I trap the left hand and bring it up. I kneel with one knee on the top of the suspect's shoulder by the top of the arm socket, my right foot planted firmly on the pavement. I see Sellers standing behind Pat, watching what is going on. We are still having problems with the right arm. So I hold the top part of the wrist and bend it. Applying pressure, I lock his arm against my right thigh. At this time a small crowd was forming, Officer Lawson is keeping the crowd back. Hodge is working to get the right arm out with his nightstick, but he's having some trouble. I reach over and grab the nightstick, and shove it in correctly. Hodge takes over and levers it, the right hand comes out, we bring the palms together, and Pats' handcuffs go on him.

We hear sirens approaching, one of the officers on scene advises that the responding cars can slow down. We may have the suspect handcuffed, but we still need to secure him in a cruiser. We don't want to cancel the assistance just yet.

"Let's get this guy up and in the car," Pat says.

However, our cars are 150 feet from the fight scene, back at Sam's Carry Out. Golf Manor, a neighboring department, was on scene for the assistance run, so we asked if we could put the suspect in their car until we can bring ours over. They agree. Sellers, Caton and I reach down to pick the suspect up. When we get him stood up, he has his feet bent up so we would have to carry him. We tell him twice to put his feet down before he complies. I look around and I see how many officers are now on scene, and I'm disgusted that we didn't have more help in subduing the suspect. I am mainly outraged at Hunter, who did nothing until Pat had to basically order him to spray the mace.

As soon as we take our first steps toward the car, with Pat and Sellers on one side, and myself on the other, Hunter steps in and tells me that he will take it from here. I let him slide in my spot and the three of them take the suspect to the car. During the foot pursuit, I lost my cuffs and nightstick, so I went to retrieve my gear. I found my nightstick under the car that we had slammed into, and my cuffs were in front of the store. When I turn around, I see that the suspect is in the back seat of the Golf Manor car, and Pat is canceling the assistance run over the radio.

Now all the release of the endorphins take over and I have to take some time to collect myself. That's when Officer Spellen walks up to me and says, "What happened dog?"

"MOVE," is my only response as I walked past him.

I like Spellen. In fact, I was his field training officer. But I don't want to be bothered right now. Everybody handles the aftermath of a struggle differently, and I need a minute or two to let my body and mind settle down. After that, I will be fine. Pat yells to me from across the parking lot to see if I had the keys to our car. When I tell him that they are in the car, he hustles over to drive it to the Sunoco lot so we can transfer the prisoner and let the Golf Manor car leave.

Officer Hodge approaches me and asks if I'm injured. He notices blood on my left shirt sleeve, and asks if it is mine? Unsure, we walk to the rear of his car, and he pours peroxide on my arm, then takes out his knife and cuts my sleeve off by the shoulder. Because blood is a contaminant, this was a smart thing to do. We discover that I am not bleeding. When Pat arrived at the Sunoco station with our cruiser I place the sleeve in the trunk to secure it. While this is going on Pat gets on his radio and requests a supervisor for a macing. Any time an officer uses force or his chemical irritant, that officer needs to report the use to his supervisor as soon as the suspect is secure.

Sergeant Watts is the only shift supervisor I had contact with. Actually I don't remember any other supervisors being there. I was told later there were others on scene. Sergeant Watts comes up to me and inquires about what went on. I start at the beginning. I explain everything to him, why the suspect was stopped, and how I had his head wrapped during the struggle. Hunter is standing next to me. When I am finished with my version, Hunter takes over. He explains to Sergeant Watts that this is the suspect who ran from him during a drug investigation a few weeks ago. Half-way into Hunter's explanation, Sergeant Watts asks who the suspect is, and where Pat is. I advise the Sergeant that the suspect's name is Owensby and Pat is by the car.

When we arrive at the Golf Manor car, the Sergeant tells the Golf Manor officer there that he is going to ask the suspect a few questions. Sergeant Watts knocks on the window and sees that the suspect is lying in a con-torted position. We all look at each other.

"Can he breathe like that?" the Sergeant asks the Golf Manor officer.

The Sergeant opens the door and taps the suspect on the shoulder. No response. We immediately go into first responder mode. Pat starts dragging Owensby out of the car as Officer Hasse retrieves a mouthpiece for CPR.

We are on the radio with the fire department, but we don't wait for them to arrive. We start CPR right away. Pat is doing the chest compressions, and Hasse, who is a trained EMT, is doing the mouth work. During compressions, Owensby coughs up something, and to this day I don't know for sure what it was. But based on my knowledge, it looked like flaky pieces of crack cocaine. Pat, being on the ball, does a mouth sweep to see if there is anything else blocking Owensby's airway. Officer's Hasse and Hodge collect the coughed up substance and place it into a property envelope.

The fire department arrives and takes over for the officers. Owensby is placed into an ambulance and I am told that they do not have a pulse and that it didn't look good for him. The area is cordoned off. I am told to sit in my cruiser and not to have contact with anyone. There is a policy in place to ensure that after a critical incident, all the officers involved are secured indi-vidually just in case they did something wrong to keep them from getting their stories to match. Interestingly enough, as soon as it became obvious that there was a medical need, officer Hunter took officer Sellers behind the Sunoco store and returned about five minutes later.

I sat in my car with all kinds of thoughts running through my head. I couldn't reason how a typical arrest could end up like this. Why is this happening? My mind was replaying the fight as I was told by my supervisor that he had gotten word from the fire company that Owensby had died. A jolt of emotion went through me, mostly confusion.

Depicts plastic bag containing marijuana, two plastic bags containing crack cocaine, one empty plastic bag and one cigar removed from the person of Roger Owensby at University Hospital by E.R. nurse 11-07-00. Taken by Senior Criminalist Lawson 11-08-00. Case # 00-PI-04

9

CHKLST

THE UNIVERSITY HOSPITAL
Social Work Department
OFFICE OF DECEDENT AFFAIRS CHECKLIST

3/27/71
Owensby, Roger
45224
4033018

TUH-806, 11/99

Date 11/7/00   Time of Call 9:00
RN _____
Pronouncing Physician Dr Bullard
Pager # _____ Date/Time of Death: 11/7   20:47
Death Cert. by: Coroner   Lic#_____
Notification of Family: ☐ present
☑ per phone: at 9:10 p by Moody
☐ in process (see Notes)
Coroner's Case: ☑ Yes ☐ No
☑ Notified at _____ by _____
☑ Coroner Accepts ☐ Coroner Declines
LifeCenter called at 11/7 9:30 1493457
                    date/time   rep.
☐ LifeCenter Accepts ☑ LifeCenter Declines
Belongings accounted for: ☐ Yes ☐ No
Valuables List signed: ☐ Yes ☐ No
A. Designation of Funeral Home/Disposition Agent
☐ Decided (See next column)
☐ Undecided Agreed contact time: _____
☐ Funeral home contacted: _____
                              date/time
B. Autopsy Coroner
☐ Family Approved ☐ Family Declined (Go to Sec. C.)
☐ Consent form signed
☐ Pathology Dept. notified: _____
☐ Chart delivered to Pathology   date/time
☐ Body in morgue: _____
                    date/time
☐ Autopsy complete: _____
C. Donation: Not eligible date/time
☐ Family Approved   ☐ Family Declined
☐ Consent form signed
☐ Agency notified at: _____
                       date/time
☐ Body in morgue: _____
                    date/time
☐ Procedure complete: _____
D. Release of Body   date/time
      CEC
☑ Body in morgue for release at 11/8/00 12:25 p.m.
                                 date/time
☐ 2d call to FH/DispAge at _____
                            date/time
☐ Body released at _____
                     date/time
Signature/Title: Cnni Moody, LSW

white-Medical Records   yellow-Stats   pink-ODA

Next of Kin/Authorized Person:

Name Brenda Owensby
Relationship Mother
Address 6570 Monte Vista
_____
Phone# ████   Alt. Phone# _____

Funeral Home/Disposition Agent:

Name Coroner
Address _____
_____
Phone# _____

NOTES: 21 y-o, Black
Male - possible overdose.
Marijuana, crack & syringe
found near. Cardiac arrest.
Mother contacted - en route
Life Center decline due to
syringe. Coroner accepts.
Police/Homicide detective
and numerous family came.
Initially, police would not allow
family to view. Volitle situation
able to take family back 2
at a time.
_____
_____
_____
_____

8-9

10

Chapter 2

One Word

I think it was at the age of 5 when I wanted to become a cop. My family was living in England at the time. My father's business took us there. During the two-and-a-half years we lived there my father had frequent assistance in his work by the Scotland Yard. I remember him taking me along with him once, to one of his more casual meetings. I was enamored with everything that had to do with the police department. The investigator my father was working with gave me a hat that the Bobbies wore, and I was hooked. While the kids I grew up with in Fetchum, Surrey, wanted to play "knights and the castle," all I wanted to play was "cops and robbers."

When my family returned to the United States, we lived in Baltimore for two years, then came home to Cincinnati. I grew up on the west side of Cincinnati, in a suburb of middle class, hard-working people. My desire to learn about law enforcement was fed by stories from my grandfather. He was a high-ranking officer in the Bureau of Prisons, and his best friend was an FBI agent. They told great "war stories" and I was their captive audience. Those stories struck such a cord that when I was in the sixth grade I made an appointment with Chief Howard Makin, of Delhi Township, to see how I could become an officer for his department when I was old enough.

Life was typical for me. I have two older sisters and one younger sister and we were always taught to obey rules and respect authority. We attended Catholic schools, played all the grade school sports, and stayed out of trouble.

When I was 13 years old, I played football for the Cincom Tomahawks. It was a traveling football team made up of boys ages 13-15. Dick Seitz was the head coach of the team and a very influential person in my development as a kid. From the first day of practice we were told we were champions.

"Being a champion is a mind set" he would tell us.

We expected to win games because we did the necessary work in practice. I remember the first practice where coach Seitz told us that if we win a game

Me at age five in Fetchum Surey, England

STATE HIGHWAY PATROL

STATE OF OHIO
George V. Voinovich
Governor

DEPARTMENT OF PUBLIC SAFETY
Charles D. Shipley
Director

FILE NO 2PER

Warren H. Davies
Superintendent

4751 Hamilton Middletown Road
Hamilton, Ohio 45011
513/863-4606
Lieutenant R. N. Johnson
April 18, 1995

Dear Sir or Madam: *Reference Robert B. Jorg*

As commander of the Hamilton Post of the Ohio State Highway Patrol I have become closely associated with Robert (Blaine) Jorg. Blaine is a active member of the Highway Patrol Auxiliary Program and he has distinguished himself as one of our finest members. He possesses all of the characteristics that are essential to excel as a police officer. Blaine is honest, dependable, intelligent , and he is a self motivator.

Blaine exercises sound judgement and he adapts well to any situation. He gets along well with his peers, supervisors, and the public. Blaine possesses solid verbal and written communication skills and he responds well to advise.

I am confident Blaine would be an outstanding asset to your department. I believe he would be a loyal, dedicated and hard working officer who would follow your department procedure as he served the citizens of Cincinnati.

Sincerely,

Lieutenant R. N. Johnson
Hamilton Post Commander

13

DELHI TOWNSHIP, OHIO

POLICE DEPARTMENT
934 Neeb Road
Delhi Township
Cincinnati, Ohio 45233

Emergency Phone   513/825-2280
Police Department   513/922-0060

March 13, 1995

TO: WHOM IT MAY CONCERN:

As a person who has known the Jorg family for a number of years, I have no hesitation in recommending
Blaine Jorg for admission to the police academy. He has the attributes necessary to become a competent
police officer. Upon completion of the police academy, I am confident he will be successful in finding
employment in his chosen field as he is the type of individual police agencies are anxious to employ when
they have the necessary opening.

Please feel free to contact me if I can offer further assistance.

Sincerely,

Howard R. Makin
HOWARD R. MAKIN
Chief of Police

14

and play it sloppy, we will practice after the game. If we lose, but gave it all we had, we would celebrate.

I played for the Tomahawks for three years. I learned even more about life than I did about football. We had several practices that would turn into team meetings. Coach Seitz would not just work our bodies into shape. He shaped our personalities. He gave his teams an education that can't have a price put on it. When we did finally get around to football, each kid on the team had to know every position on every play.

"You're only as strong as your weakest player," he would say.

I remember the practice before our big game with the Central Trust Vikings. We practiced for three hours and never once touched a football. We sat under a picnic shelter and orally reviewed every play: how to block, tackle, run, etc. On that game day, the Vikings ran the opening kickoff for a touchdown. Our team pulled together to discuss what went wrong and how we had to work together to keep it from happening again. The opposing team never had another positive yard, and we won 41-7.

We were taught about respect and being equals on the team and in life. Coach Seitz developed our characters as well as our athletic ability. In the three years I played under him, we never lost a game.

I wasn't the best of students most of my school career, but I finished strong in high school. I went to an all boys' Catholic school, the pride of the west side, Elder High School. I learned how to live as a true Christian, letting my belief in God show through in everything I do. The teachers there taught me leadership, partnership, and the value of community service. In fact, community service was expected of us. The school motto was one simple word, Altiora, which is Latin for "the higher things."

After graduating from Elder High School, I attended the University of Cincinnati to pursue a degree in criminal justice. At the university, my instructor for Vehicle Patrol Techniques was a state trooper with the Ohio State Patrol. He could tell I was highly motivated to become an officer. He advised me that the highway patrol was hiring for auxiliary troopers. Volunteering was just fine with me. It was something they taught us to love at Elder. After qualifying for a position, I went through the academy and graduated in April, 1992. I worked out of Post nine in Butler County by night, attended college by day, and worked for the university in between.

The troopers at Post nine taught me more than I could retain. I was quizzed more in the cruiser than I was in the classroom. It was the best training they could have given me.

The job working at the university's telephone fundraising department turned out to be important, too. It was there that I met a man who would help me through a criminal trial and a woman who would get me through the five years of hell that followed.

Brian had a wicked sense of humor. He's a sound effects kind of guy. We used to sit together at work and laugh through most of the shift. We were roommates. We were brothers.

Kristen was my supervisor at work and I admired her a lot. She is kind-hearted and honest. If you don't want a straight answer, be careful what you ask her. She had a thing about dating people at work so we didn't start dating until she graduated college and got another job. The first time I asked her out, she turned me down. I won her over, though. And we would be engaged before I graduated.

I was newly married and out of school when I saw an ad for police officers for the city of Cincinnati. It took a year, but I went through the recruiting process and in January, 1996, I entered the police academy. The 81st recruit class graduated on June 6, 1996. I was assigned to District Two, second relief, 3pm-11pm. When I completed my field training, I spent another six months in District Two. Then I was transferred to District Four. My first assignment was in the community of Hartwell, in the north side of the district, bordering other jurisdictions.

I had been working for about a year when a friend of mine, Scott Hughes, then a Village of Greenhills officer, asked me to assist him with training recruits at the Butler County Police Training Academy. He was volunteering in an officer/suspect contact course and wanted me to help enact scenarios. Man, I loved it! I was able to see through the eyes of 30 different recruits, six instructors and even suspects by acting out real life situations from the street. I was learning as much as I was teaching. When the classes were over, I talked to the head instructor who invited me back for the next class and I continued to volunteer at the academy until the thirteen minutes that turned my life over and inside-out.

Back in Cincinnati, I became a bike officer in the fall of my second year. I remained in District Four, but I was relocated to beat three, Avondale, and I was partnered up with Shawn "the machine" George. He is the only officer I have ever met who chased a car on his bike and caught it. Shawn opened my eyes to a side of policing that I hadn't seen much of: street-level drug enforcement. I had made drug arrests in the past, but now I was being educated by one of the city's best beat officers. He taught me all of the "ins and outs" of the drug trade. We spent several days learning about surveillance, how to approach suspects, everything. I liked working with Shawn a great deal.

I returned to Hartwell in the spring of 1997, because Shawn had been assigned as a neighborhood officer in Avondale. I wasn't looking to partner up with anyone at the time. I was enjoying being by myself again. That's when I met Pat Caton. I was working from 3pm to 11pm. Pat was working 9pm to 5am. We would only work together for two hours a night and only handle a few runs together, but there was something I liked about how he did his job. Pat was very respectful to all citizens, whether your car broke down on the side of the road, and you just needed to use a phone to call someone, or he was arresting you. Pat is the constant professional. The radio runs we handled together seemed to go very smoothly, so we talked about partnering up. We knew that if we did, we would be working Bond Hill. That year, Bond Hill had seen more drug runs, violent crime, and homicides than any other part of the city. That didn't phase us. We knew we could work anywhere together.

There is just something about Pat, a tough-as-nails Irishman. Pat is a former Marine Captain, and he has a mouth on him. He has such a grasp of the English language, he could tell you how to tie your shoes and you'd be on the edge of your seat waiting to see how it turns out. He is a man of high integrity, a man who would do anything for anybody.

Pat grew up in the same neighborhood as I did. Only his neighborhood was in Detroit. We had the same parental structure and discipline, went to the same kind of schools and were taught the same values. Pat and I grew up together, but in two different places.

Immediately after we started working together, we flew. Things just worked smoothly. We knew what each other was thinking, and how the other was going to react in most situations. I trusted Pat with everything. I trusted Pat with my life.

Everyone must submit himself to the governing authorities, for there is no authority except that which God has established. The authorities that exist have been established by God. Consequently, he who rebels against the authority is rebelling against what God has instituted, and those who do so will bring judgment on themselves. For the rulers hold no terror for those who do right, but for those who do wrong. Do you want to be free from fear of the one authority? Then do what is right and he will commend you. For he is God's servant to do you good. But if you do wrong, be afraid, for he does not bear the sword for nothing. He is God's servant, an agent of wrath to bring punishment on the wrongdoer. Therefore, it is necessary to submit to the authorities, not only because of possible punishment but also of conscience.

Romans 13:1-5

We shared the same desire to be the best officers we could be. We worked hard to be ready for any situation that arose. When Pat became a bike officer, we would go to the target range at least once a month with our bikes. We would ride our bikes about a mile and a half, right up to the firing line, and engage the targets. Then we got back on the bikes, rode to the point that we were almost dizzy, and then approached the line again. We would go through different scenarios. If there was someone at the range who knew more than we did, we would ask them for pointers. We weren't the best cops on the force, but we wanted to be, and we would pick the brains of those who were willing to teach us.

Pat and I continued to seek out training anywhere we could find it. I still volunteered at the police academy, and brought back information I learned. We were a great team. The entire time I worked with Pat I never second-guessed anything we did. On the streets we did everything by the book. On our way back from the jail, we would review what we had been through. Many times we questioned how we survived a situation, how we got lucky. But I don't think it was luck, I think that Pat and I took our job so seriously that we had the ability to handle the worst of situations.

We took that attitude to every facet of our job. One day when Pat was off, I was asked by Charlie Dukes, the Roselawn community officer, if I could come up to the residents' community meeting. I really didn't want to at first, I didn't want to take away time from the street patrols, but I went. I was amazed at how many people wanted to talk to me about problems in their neighborhood. When you are on the street working, most people don't want to talk to you. They want to get away from you. I wasn't used to residents who wanted to talk.

When Pat came back to work, I told him about my experience and when the next meeting approached, I told Pat that we should go. We got there right in the middle of Charlie's presentation. When we sat down, Charlie paused to introduce Pat. He went into a story about the last time he saw Pat: "You all know Officer Jorg. This is his partner, Officer Caton. The last time I saw Officer Caton, he was wrestling a man with a gun who was trying to rob someone at an ATM machine." Pat received a standing ovation. That day gave us a connection to our beat we never had before.

We took the information the residents gave us and integrated it into our patrol duties. The community responded well to our involvement. We went to all the community meetings we were able. We also brought other officers with us. We wanted to be part of the community and truly serve it. We gained the respect of the community residents. It felt like they became "our" residents. We worked hard, and it paid off.

Just as we felt like these residents were ours, the neighborhood became ours as well. The drug dealers and gang members stopped yelling out "Police!" as we approached. It was "CatonandJorg!". -That's right, one word. If you saw one, you knew the other was not far behind.

Chapter 3
"Chokehold Gone Bad"

Standard procedure puts all officers involved in a critical incident on administrative leave. While we were off work for seven days, we went to mandatory counseling and regrouped.

The death of Roger Owensby fueled anger throughout City Hall, and it was about to get worse. That Wednesday, November 8, during a city council meeting members of the Black United Front and Black Baptist Ministers were present. They demanded to know what happened that night and what the cause of Owensby's death was. It was either Councilman Paul Booth or his assistant who called the coroner during the meeting for an answer to the death of Mr. Owensby. Mr. Booth announced to the assembly. "Asphyxiation, a choke hold gone bad, piling on, or both."

The information given to Mr. Booth was the coroner's pre-autopsy estimation, concluded in 18 hours after the death. The information that the coroner used was the external injuries on Roger Owensby, and what he was told by the Homicide unit. At this point no internal examination of the body had been done. Sergeant Carter, the lead investigator, told the coroner that there was vomit found at the scene of the struggle. He also said that Lieutenant Luebbe was told by Sergeant Browner that there was a choke hold used. Neither piece of information was correct.

The general theme in the meeting was "A cop must go to jail." The press wasted no time reporting the sensational findings, and the bandwagon was quickly filling up. When I was watching the news that day, I could not believe what I was seeing. I was dumbfounded. I picked up the phone and called Pat right away. Neither one of us could understand how this conclusion of a chokehold or piling on was being made.

Hamilton County Assistant Coroner, Dr. Daniel Schultz, who actually performed the autopsy, decided that Owensby had died on the ground at the fight scene. He based his findings on two pieces of evidence: the place he was told the vomit was found --The last thing a person's body will do when deprived of oxygen is vomit -- and how long the struggle had lasted. He was told that it lasted two minutes.

CARL L. PARROTT, JR., M.D.

HAMILTON COUNTY CORONER

The Frank P. Cleveland, M.D. Institute of Forensic Medicine, Toxicology and Criminalistic

3159 Eden Avenue, Cincinnati, Ohio 45219-2299   Main Office: 513-221-4524

Fax: 513-221-0307   Crime Laboratory: 513-221-4528   Morgue: 513-221-4529

November 8, 2000

PRESS RELEASE

Roger Owensby was pronounced dead within minutes of arrival at the University of Cincinnati Medical Center last evening following a physical confrontation with police officers who were attempting to arrest him. An autopsy was performed this morning and the cause of death is mechanical asphyxia. The coroner's investigation is not complete, in that toxicological and other studies remain pending.

Dr. Parrott will be available at 2:00 PM today.

On November 19, 2000, well after the press and the vocal minority decided that the coroner's pre-autopsy statement was gospel, the coroner, Dr. Carl Parrott, finally had the toxicology report. At that time he seemed unsure as to the cause of death.

Dr. Parrott then said, "Until the investigation is complete, it will be impossible to know for certain how Mr. Owensby died... it gets real complicated, we've got a tangle of events here."

Dr. Parrott's analysis of the body tissue and his medical findings gave reason to question the cause of death. But that wasn't what the public wanted to hear.

Dr. Schultz said that, "a constellation of things" led him to reach the asphyxiation conclusion. "Number one, he doesn't have any other reason to be deceased... He didn't die from a drug overdose -- didn't die from some natural underlying cause," he said. Dr. Schultz also admitted that in making a ruling he also considers, "Things that I find out from circumstances, I take it all into context."

In reading all the witness interrogations from the homicide unit, there was not one person who witnessed a chokehold, civilian or police. It didn't stop the press from taking liberty with this information and running with "chokehold" for two weeks. After the coroner announced his findings, the homicide unit realized that they didn't have a witness who could corroborate this information. They needed to find one.

A seventeen-year-old girl who, by her own admission, has been smoking marijuana for the past eight years, became that witness. On the night of the seventh, Aerial St. Clair was questioned extensively about what she saw. But she never said it was a chokehold.

She claimed that the officers beat Owensby to death.

My seven-day leave was close to an end when I received a call from my lieutenant. She advised me that I was going to stay on paid administrative leave for a few more days until this matter was cleared up. I called my Fraternal Order of Police appointed attorney, Don Hardin, and asked him why I wasn't able to go back to work. This was unprecedented. I wanted to get back on the street. My attorney advised me that until this matter was taken care of, the chief thought it would be wise for all the officers involved to stay off the streets.

I had a difficult time trying to understand. I stayed in my house most of the time. It was probably the worst thing I could have done. All I did was watch the news. I was on T.V. -on every channel. So I turned on the radio instead. It was there, too.

The days grew harder to deal with. The only information I received seemed to be worse than the last. Then one day I received a call from my FOP attorney. He wanted me to meet him at his office. That is never good news. When I arrived, I saw Pat there as well. As we talked in the lobby Mr. Hardin greeted us, then brought us back to his conference room. We were informed that our case was going to go in front of a grand jury, and that we were going to need to hire legal representation.

My heart sunk into my chest as I heard the news. I could see the concern in Pats face as well. I felt like I stood in front of Mr. Hardin for an hour before I could say anything. I had so many questions going through my head, but I couldn't speak. Mr. Hardin advised us that Pat and I were the only two officers involved in the grand jury investigation.

I went with Pat back to his house to talk about this new development. I must admit I don't remember any of the conversation. The realization that we may face a prison sentence for doing our job was, to say the least, unnerving. We ourselves still didn't understand why Owensby was dead.

The following day was Roger Owensby's funeral. Reverend Leslie Isaiah Gaines, Jr. was reported in a news paper as saying, "If it causes some friends of Roger's to quit selling drugs, then his life will not have been in vain."

The Reverend may not have come right out and said Owensby was selling drugs, but he certainly understood that Owensby was associated with people who did.

Mr. Owensby did have past drug related encounters with police. In December of 1999, he pleaded guilty to possession of drugs. This information would be part of the "tangle of events" Dr. Parrott referred to.

September 27, 2000, I was working surveillance with Officer Hunter. We were in a parking lot across the street from Sam's Carry Out, watching multiple drug transactions. Three people were involved; one would start the conversation, one would take the money, and one would hand over the narcotic. We observed for 45 minutes or more, waiting for a marked car to become available. When one was on its way, we gave the information to the officers about the vehicle and a description of the driver. As the police car went to stop the buyer, Hunter and I approached the sellers. As soon as we got out of our car, the suspect who was carrying the drugs ran. Hunter gave chase. I stayed with the other two suspects, taking them into custody. Hunter was calling out the foot pursuit, so other police officers could assist him in the apprehension. About five minutes into the pursuit, Hunter advised over the radio that he had lost visual contact of the suspect and that he was returning to Sam's.

I placed the two subjects I had under arrest for criminal trespassing, read them their Miranda rights, then asked them who the man was who ran. They claimed that they only know his street name, "L.A." When Hunter returned to Sam's, he advised me that during the chase, he caught up with the suspect, and that the suspect assaulted him. We put out the description again, but since we could not locate the individual after a reasonable amount of time, we had to leave to process the two prisoners.

On October 13, 2000, Owensby was a passenger in a vehicle that was stopped by Officers Butler and Davis at 4:59 am. Officer Davis noticed an odor of marijuana on or about the person of Owensby. The officer found nine cellophane bags of marijuana along with a plastic baggie of hashish. Owensby was arrested for preparation of drugs with the intent to sell. In addition, he had a cell phone, a pager and $337 in cash. Mr. Owensby informed the officers when asked about his employment status, that he was unemployed.

On November 7, 2000, Owensby had on his person five ounces of crack cocaine and 26 grams of marijuana.

For whatever reason, the information of the drugs found in Owensby's pockets was swept under the rug. Neither the police department nor the media seemed to have any interest in looking into Owensby's past or any other information that could have contributed to his death.

Attitudes and opinions were continually offered by the media. Most of it was inaccurate and hateful. Pat and I were faced with a bizarre reality. All we could do at this point was wait.

Chapter 4
Attitudes and Opinions

Each day brought a new development. In this case, none of them good. Every time a development came out, there was another snippet on the news. The idea of police brutality continued to attract attention.

Reverend Damon Lynch III, long time pastor of the New Jerusalem Baptist Church in Cincinnati, and president of the Black United Front, made headlines when he proclaimed that Owensby was chased only because he was black and might have looked like a suspect who was wanted. Lynch also said that I had, "killed this man with a marine-style chokehold." It was a terribly inaccurate and inflammatory thing to say. It caused me considerable grief... and fear. After Lynch fanned the flames of hatred, I was afraid some nut would find me, or my wife. With the accusations that were being made, I didn't feel safe to leave my house. I was even afraid to go to the gas station, hearing people talking about what they were hearing on the news, and then seeing my face on the front page of the newspaper. The home that was my security was quickly becoming a jail.

Lynch distorted the facts and inflamed racial passions of the black community, but the response from Police Headquarters was just as disturbing: silence. Still no new information on the circumstances that led to the death of Roger Owensby was available. There was talk of firing the city manager. The odd thing is that even though the black minority was causing trouble, I felt more betrayed by the policymakers and the prosecutor's office. They refused to stand up and remind the public that there was no conclusive evidence yet.

The media was trying it's best to get someone from the police department to say something about the investigation. I was the someone every news journalist wanted to talk to, but I wasn't allowed to say anything. It was made clear that I was to remain silent. It was tough; I had a lot I wanted to say.

The frustration of not being able to say anything was almost overpowering. It is so hard to sit back and see your name slung through the mud. My wife, Kristen, and Pat were the only people I was talking to. There were things

I couldn't tell my family about my fears and range of emotions. Reporters would show up at my front door, I always told them the same thing: "Sorry, I can't talk to you."

I had been seeing police psychologist Dr. Daum since the day after Owensby's death. If something was bothering me, I knew I could talk to him. When I was having a bad day, I would call him up and ask when I could stop in for a visit. Dr. Daum never kept me waiting long. He was agreeable, but I'm not sure if he helped me at that time. Being able to vent to someone can be constructive, but knowing my feelings wouldn't go any further didn't help. Dr. Daum isn't a policymaker. He can't go and tell anybody how I felt, so I might as well talk to a wall.

Pressure for information from the press and the community on the investigation continued to mount. The police department promised an update on November 11, Chief Tom Streicher made a public statement that he was personally supervising every aspect of the investigation. There was nothing new. More waiting, more tension, and more rumors.

On November 14, the day the Cincinnati Enquirer carried the headline, "Officer's Silence Creates Quandary" someone finally spoke up for Pat and I. In a letter to the editor, Jay Clark, the chairperson of the Greater Cincinnati Criminal Defense Lawyers Association reminded readers that "Police have rights," He added that the presumption of innocence, right to counsel and the right to remain silent apply to all citizens.

If the media expected any answers at the next city council meeting, it was sorely disappointed. Chief Streicher reported that he still didn't know what had happened, and that nothing had been determined. The absence of witnesses didn't deter the media from perpetuating the myth that councilman Paul Booth and Reverend Lynch kept repeating: racial profiling, and a chokehold were a part of that night's occurrences. On November 15, the Cincinnati Post irresponsibly reported that, "Some witnesses said officers pressed their batons against the throat, to disable him." Also, "Other witnesses have said officers applied a chokehold to Owensby." The Post did not name these witnesses; readers had no idea who these people were, nor if they were credible.

With such misinformation being reported as the facts, I understood why the black community was outraged. I know how it must have looked: another black man dies at the hands of police. Eleven black males had been shot or killed by Cincinnati police officers between 1995 and November 7, 2000. Then within 19 hours of Owensby's death, another man, Jeffery Irons, was shot and killed by police. No wonder local politic officials, and leaders of the · black community reacted the way they did.

Saying that there was a rush to judgment would be a gross understatement. I understand that officials felt they had to react. Unfortunately, the facts were disregarded as the finger pointing and accusations flew. I was reminded of the saying, "Truth is the first causality of war." That's what happened here.

Make no mistake, the police chief and the politicians were involved in a public relations nightmare. But facts are facts. There is no benefit to changing or altering the facts. There is reality, and then there is what people sell to the community.

By the year 2000, the number of black males shot by police in Cincinnati seemed to be an epidemic. But you can't generalize; each incident needs to be weighed solely on its own merit. In the haste to hang a cop, the people who cry "police brutality" fail to consider all the circumstances that led to the deaths of individuals. Here are the facts on the eleven men who died at the hands of Cincinnati Police Officers prior to November 7th.

Harvey Price. Shot and killed by a SWAT team member on February 1, 1995, After killing his girlfriend's fifteen year-old daughter with an axe. Price kept police at bay for hours. He was shot when he approached officers with a raised knife.

Darryll Price. Died April 4, 1996, from agitated delirium with restraint, after a scuffle with police. The incident began because Price, who was high on cocaine, was beating on a car in traffic, threatening to shoot someone. When police arrived, a scuffle ensued. Price was handcuffed and shackled, yet continued to struggle as rescue workers attempted to administer first aid for his cuts and abrasions. He suddenly stopped moving, and died within an hour.

Lorenzo Collins. Died February 23, 1997, five days after being shot by police. Collins, who had a history of mental illness, escaped from University Hospital. He was chased by police, when he eventually was cornered, he threatened police with a brick, he was shot twice.

Daniel Williams. Died February 2, 1998. Williams shot Officer Kathleen Conway four times with a .357 Magnum at point-blank range in an unprovoked attack before Conway could return fire and kill him. Williams had previous convictions for domestic violence and felonious assault.

Jermaine Lowe. Died June 3,1998. Lowe shot at police after he crashed a car he had stolen. Officers who had been pursuing the stolen vehicle shot him. There was an outstanding warrant for his arrest for armed robbery when the incident occurred.

Randy Black. Died July 17, 1998. Black was wielding a 2x4 pierced with nails when an officer shot him. The incident occurred after Black robbed a credit union with a handgun. Black fled when police arrived on the scene, tossing his handgun away and grabbing the 2x4 when he was cornered.

Michael Carpenter. Died March 19,1999. A police officer standing behind Carpenter's car fired nine shots into the vehicle when he saw the car's back up lights come on. Carpenter had just dragged an officer who was trying to pull Carpenter out of the car. The incident occurred during a traffic stop. Carpenter, who was driving with expired tags, refused to exit the car when ordered by the police. He then reached for the glove compartment, which is when the officer reached in and grabbed the driver, who then drove 15 feet, stopped and put the car in reverse.

James King. Died August 20, 1999. King committed armed robbery at a bank, then sped away with the police in pursuit. He ditched his car when he hit a dead-end, but then refused to drop his weapon when ordered by police. Officers shot and killed him.

Carey Tompkins. Died October 16, 1999. Tompkins was shot by an officer who responded to a 9-1-1 call from Tompkins' apartment. The dispatcher who received the call heard the girl's father asking an angry Tompkins why he brought a gun and pointed it at his daughter. Tompkins had a gun in his waistband when he met police at the door. A struggle ensued, and Tompkins was shot.

Alfred Pope. Died March 14, 2000. Pope, who had beaten and robbed three people earlier in the day, pointed his gun at police who responded to a call from a citizen who heard shots being fired. Pope's rap sheet included eighteen felony charges. Police shot several shots and killed Pope.

Courtney Mathis. Died September 1, 2000. This bizarre incident began when twelve year old Mathis stole a car. When a police officer at a convience store asked to see his driver's license, Mathis slammed his car into reverse. the officer reached into the car trying to turn the ignition key, or grab the gear shift. After being dragged five hundred feet, the officer managed to shoot the driver in the chest. Officer Crayon died after hitting his head, Mathis died several hours later.

In 2003, there were seventy-six homicides in the city of Cincinnati; most of them were black-on-black crime. In the past five years, there were thirteen people who were killed by Cincinnati officers. Cincinnati officers are walking into situations where they are now scared to pull their weapons if they need to. Cops are afraid to use the appropriate amount of force when the situation calls for it, because it may cost them everything they have worked so hard for. All because they are afraid that they will not be supported.

In my case, city leaders painted a picture of police brutality and sold it over and over to the public. Crime increased dramatically, arrests dropped, countless law-abiding citizens moved out of a now-unsafe city, and morale in the police department hit an all-time low. In Cincinnati, there were one hundred murders in a three year period from 1998-2000. In the next two years, murder jumped to one hundred ninety-four, an increase of eighty percent. Robberies rose approximately eighty percent, burglaries went up twenty-five percent, and auto theft rose one hundred-ten percent. With such a dramatic increase in violent crime, it stands to reason that arrests would be up as well. The opposite is true. Arrests and contacts dropped about 110,000 or fifty-seven percent after Pat and I were indicted.

No one at city hall would admit that criminals were taking over the streets. Instead, politicians tried to put a positive spin on the numbers, saying that violent crime decreased 7.4 percent in the first half of 2003. They just failed to mention that violent crime was up in 2002. The sad part is that the decline in the statistics was blamed on a police slowdown, allegedly issued by the FOP. Keith Fangman, President of the FOP, never issued a slowdown. He merely issued an advisory. Use extreme caution and think twice before engaging in self-initiated activity that could put you in a situation that may require using force.

Even the Cincinnati Enquirer could see that the police had been handcuffed. On May 15, 2001, the Enquirer editorial read, "Police! Fewer Arrests." The article noted a down-turn in arrests, that the jail population decreased by about one hundred in ten days. The Enquirer listed possible reasons why: Cops are afraid of being dragged into federal lawsuits alleging racial profiling. Cops are discouraged by criticism and lack of support.

The Department of Justice came to Cincinnati to review the police department in 2001. After months of inquiries, the city instituted new policies and procedures. Police officers became bogged down with needless paperwork. It was one knee jerk reaction after another. An agreement ended a lawsuit brought on by the Black United Front and other civil activists that alleged decades of discrimination against blacks; and a memorandum outlining changes in the police use of force, training, record keeping and dealing with the community. Many officers worried about the new reporting requirements, contact cards that needed to be filled out every time an officer had contact with a subject in a traffic stop, to keep track of how many people of each race were being stopped, and for what. Officers said they feared punishment if their use of force numbers got too high. No one knew how high was too high.

Chapter 5

From the Lips of a Pot Head

To an outsider, it looked like police weren't trying to find out why Roger Owensby, Jr. had died. The truth is that chief Streicher's Homicide detectives were trying tremendously hard to find out what they could pin on someone - anyone. It was as if they were trying to fit a square peg into a round hole.

On November 15, 2000, prosecutor Mike Allen finally said the magic words that Rev. Damon Lynch, councilman Paul Booth, and the NAACP wanted to hear: that the police officers involved in the arrest of Roger Owensby, Jr. would likely face a grand jury.

The announcement confirmed what many had believed all along: that Owensby had died because of police misconduct. Never mind that grand juries don't determine guilt or innocence; they only determine whether sufficient evidence exists to proceed with a case in the court system. Most people assume that a prosecutor wouldn't call a grand jury unless he or she had a concrete case. In this case, nothing could be farther from the truth.

On the surface, it appeared that Sergeant Carters' investigators were leaving no stone unturned in their quest for the truth. After all, thirteen homicide detectives would interview twenty-eight members of the police department, and seven civilian "witnesses." With all that questioning, you would think they would find the truth. And I believe they did.

But the truth never reached the grand jury, nor the public. It was discarded and disregarded because it didn't fit the scenario that had already gained public acceptance. That became crystal clear when I read the transcripts of the interviews with "witnesses."

The Homicide investigation was flawed from the get-go. Detectives were convinced that I did something very wrong before they asked a single question. It's obvious from the leading questions they asked to the District Four police officers: "What rumors did you hear around the district?" And, "Tell me of the rumors you've heard."

Officer Don Brown answered, "Only information we got was from the newspaper. Especially the asphyxiation stuff."

Officer Jeremy Howard replied, "Everything you've seen in the news." His comment was followed by laughter in the interview room. He continued, "From the fact that they were jumping on his chest to the fact it was a simple arrest and he choked on crack."

Officer Robert Orchard responded, "That there was a struggle. The suspect was placed in back of the car. I heard he was conscious, he was fine when they placed him in the back of the car. I got this info from Hasse, Konicki and Howard. We learned from the news which officers were involved." He added, "I don't even know why I'm here (for the interview)."

Officer Don Konicki said, "He had drugs on him and he ran."

Officer Rick Hoskins told detectives, "I'm in the dark on this other than what you hear on the news. I haven't heard any rumors."

Officer Tammy Schneider was asked, 'What's being said around the district? I mean this has to be a major point of discussion around the district."

Her reply, "I haven't heard anything other than they were gonna start presenting evidence to the grand jury."

Detective: "What about the rumors to how the guy died?"

Her answer, "Nothing."

If detectives would have spent less time trying to confirm rumors and more time listening to facts, they would have picked up important information that not only would have cleared me, but would have shed light on the truth behind Owensby's death. Set aside the rumors for a moment, and consider what these witnesses were telling detectives: "He was conscious... he was fine when placed in the car... he had drugs... he ran... Why didn't they explore why Lt. Roy Higgins, said, "Sgt. Meyer called me. Said the emergency (guy) said it was a classic heart attack."

And then there was Captain Mike Curreton, who told detectives, "Lieutenant told me it was a heart attack." If only the detectives had listened, they would have reached the unshakable conclusion that the five arresting officers did not violate police policy, commit a criminal act, or abuse Roger Owensby, Jr. If they hadn't already decided that Owensby died because an officer choked him or that officers "piled on", they might have realized Owensby died from an adrenaline rush, or choked on something he had put in his mouth, that he may have ingested crack cocaine.

That scenario was certainly staring them in the face. Consider what officers told the detectives. Officer Alexander: "I was down there with the body at the (hospital), All this time I thought this guy swallowed crack, maybe choked on crack. When I heard this extra stuff (chokehold gone bad, piling on) I'm like Man, where did this come from? I know these guys and I know they wouldn't intentionally hurt anybody, wouldn't intentionally try to do anybody harm."

Officer Hasse: "... once Fire was on the scene and took over, I noticed a crack-like substance on the subject's chin and cheek. Myself and Officer Hodge secured the substance and placed it in a property envelope ... During CPR, when I had placed the mask on him every time I would blow in a breath, I would hear a gurgling as the air expired back out. So I could tell the airway was blocked. I saw what I thought, 'this is crack that came out of his airway' (as Fire Department was using the suctioning device to clear his airway)."

Sergeant Julie Shearer: "When I walked up to Hasse, I could see that Mr. Owensby had some type of white substance on his face. I gathered up a little bit and Hasse put it in an evidence envelope ... (Caton) advised me that he had a pen that he tried to clear Mr. Owensby's airway with."

Captain David Ratliff: "When they pulled him out of the car (per Hasse) the prisoner regurgitated or threw up a wad of white stuff on his shoulder. There was crack cocaine found on the prisoner. It was my belief that had some, possibly some kind of drugs, that would've had some bearing on his death... I know from the supervisors that work with these officers, they're four good officers."

Sergeant Pete Watts: "He was laying on his left side. Officer Hodge was giving him medical attention and he said, a foamy white substance was emitted from his mouth. He took the gauze and preserved it. Cause he thought it might have been cocaine."

Officer Jason Hodge: "...looked like they put a suction hose down his throat ...white flakes came out of his mouth. I told Hasse, 'Go get me a property envelope.' I recovered those flakes. I thought it was crack cocaine or something. I thought he might have swallowed something when I saw those flakes, the yellowish/white flakes. That's why I recovered them. I thought, 'Well maybe, maybe this guy swallowed crack and had stopped his heart or something.'"

In all, eight interviewees mentioned seeing or hearing about a white flaky substance on or near Roger Owensby after he was removed from the police cruiser and resuscitation efforts were underway. But detectives didn't want to talk about the "white' flaky substance." Every time someone mentioned what came out of Owensby's mouth, detectives changed the subject. They didn't ask one follow-up question.

You would think all that talk about a suspect vomiting a white, flaky substance would lead detectives to explore the possibility that Owensby had ingested crack cocaine. Sergeant Anthony Carter and his investigators didn't pursue such a vital piece of the puzzle. Nor did they interview the six EMT personnel who responded to the scene and worked on Owensby.

Instead detectives lead and intimidated honest cops. Case in point: Officer Jason Hodge answered all their questions, but his answers weren't the answers they wanted. So they used bullying and veiled threats throughout the interview in an attempt to receive the responses they were looking for. Here are a few of the most disturbing things detectives said to Officer Hodge:

"I don't wanna preach to you. But I don't wanna see you jammed up over minimal involvement in this. I'm sure (your attorney) Mr. Hardin told you this is going to the grand jury. And I'd hate to see you get jammed up in this... This is a homicide investigation. And it's important that everybody tells everything they know... And it's my opinion, for what's it worth, that you're telling me your involvement but there's a lot more to this than you're telling us... Not just your involvement but observations, what you heard. Not so much what you did but you saw other guys do, what you heard 'em say afterwards ... And every officer is gonna have to stand up and raise their right hand and swear to tell the truth... and I would hate to see any of the officers involved in this get jammed up by the... you know, there's a time for officers to look out for each other. Okay. But this is the time where we have we're involved in a death investigation. This is a homicide investigation."

On and on it went with the detectives strong-arming Hodge: "I hear what you're telling us... But I think you're leaving out things... Obviously something happened more than you're telling us you saw and observed and heard and talked to officers... You obviously know what's been in the papers and what the coroner's saying on this? ... There has to be some logical explanation for what happened to this guy. It's hard for me to imagine that you guys didn't talk about what happened, just naturally being cops ... It's my impression, and that of my partners too, that you maybe leaving some important things out. Okay this guy didn't die from being handcuffed... It's hard for me to believe that you don't hear what's going on around you. The first thing is everybody says what happened. We're curious. We want to know. We wanna know the dirt... You're still saying that there was no conversation about what happened that night right there in front of Sam's ... And just so you know-and I wanna be extremely clear on this so on down the road we don't have a problem, the interviews that we've done, the video tapes that we've looked at, the sound broadcasts, the radio communications that we have, do not match up with what you're telling us."

How many different ways are there to call someone a liar? I'm proud Officer Hodge kept his composure.

Detectives also wrestled with Lieutenant Steve Luebbe who wisely brought his original notes from the incident to his interview. Detectives really hammered him after he stated that Sergeant Browner told him that, "somewhere along the line, one of the officers said they used a chokehold on the man." She must have been referring to me because I was the only officer near his neck, but I never used a chokehold. I never spoke to Sgt. Browner that night.

Later in her interview, Sergeant Browner states that she never made that comment to Lieutenant Luebbe about any use of a chokehold. Lieutenant Luebbe also revealed that Sgt. Browner said, "...we think it could be also cocaine involved. He may have swallowed some crack cocaine or something like that cause there's white substance on his shirt collar." But they weren't interested in that.

They repeatedly tried to get Officer Victor Spellen to say I used a chokehold although they called it a "neck hold," "While you were Officer Jorg's partner, you were his recruit, did he ever use any kind of restraint like that before when you guys were partners?"

Spellen's response, "No."

Later, they asked: "At any point and time did Officer Jorg ever show you any type of a chokehold, neck hold, or any type of restraint around the neck?"

Spellen, "No."

How differently things would have turned out if these so-called detectives had been as diligent about pursuing the possibility of a drug-induced heart attack as they were about trying to make officers admit to something they never saw.

Alarms and whistles should have sounded when they talked with Sergeant Steve Meyer, who told them "I was the first police officer at the hospital. Nurse showed me a bag of drugs which had what appeared to be marijuana and crack cocaine. She said she found the property on Mr. Owensby, found it in his front pocket. She showed me a little baggie that was empty, two or three bags of crack cocaine and a large bag of marijuana." Meyer also told detectives "I ask Hodge, did you see somebody hit anybody, and he said, 'No.' He said, when putting him in the car, he (Owensby) was fighting, but I don't know what he meant by that. He was moving his feet, but needed assistance." It should have been clear to detectives that Owensby didn't die at the scene of the struggle, and that he may have ingested the contents of the "empty baggie" found on his person at the hospital, It's common for drug dealers and users to hide evidence in their mouth or swallow it. There was crack cocaine residue in that baggie. But they remained fixated on the "chokehold gone bad" theory.

They should have been anxious to talk to all of the EMT workers on the scene that night, especially after Sycamore Township's Craig Coburn (who was working with the Cincinnati Fire Dept.) told them, "He had vomited ... We did notice white stuff in vomit ... To us, it was pretty much a cardiac arrest. No swelling of the neck." Coburn mentioned the names of two other paramedics with first-hand information, but detectives did not interview either person. They interviewed twenty-eight cops and came up with nothing to fit the, "rogue cop chokes suspect to death" script they are so desperately trying to sell.

Fortunately, the officers didn't go along. And for that, I'm thankful. I'm so proud of the officers who told the truth, especially considering that detectives tried to intimidate or lead them to the storyline they had adopted. I wonder what pressure was brought upon Sergeant Pete Watts, a dedicated officer District Four is fortunate to have. Obviously, his words carry great weight since he was just seconds away when the call went out and was the first boss on the scene. Sergeant Watts told detectives that no one mentioned a chokehold, stranglehold, or anything of that nature. When asked if I mentioned anything about getting Owensby in a headlock, he replied, "No." I used a maneuver called a head wrap, it is used in partnership with pressure point manipulation techniques. In order to activate a pressure point anywhere on the head, you must apply pressure and counter pressure. Simply applying pressure to a nerve will not accomplish any effect. A chokehold in this situation, a non life-threatening situation, would have been unnecessary, and illegal. He also said, "They took his shirt off. I didn't see any bruises on him or anything."

You would think that detectives would have come away from their interviews saying, "Forget the chokehold angle. It obviously didn't happen. Let's try to find out more about that white stuff Owensby coughed up." But they didn't. They were determined to take rumors and hearsay, add them to their theory, and take that package to the grand jury.

Thanks to Sergeant Carter and the Homicide detectives, we will probably never find out exactly how Roger Owensby died. Unfortunately, detectives and members of the prosecutor's office chose to advance lies instead of the truth. They had absolutely no evidence that would incriminate a Cincinnati police officer. But the politicians had already decided someone would be sacrificed.

When they realized that their "chokehold/piling on" theory didn't hold water, they should have stood up and said, "It didn't happen the way we thought." Of course, that would have opened them up to the same kind of public scorn I underwent. I think it's safe to say that the Owensby family and black community would have been screaming, "Cover-up!" if any of the investigators had been bold and honest enough to tell what they were hearing in their interviews there would have been backlash to deal with.

So they stubbornly stuck to the script. A script they can make work in front of a jury if they have an "eyewitness" or two willing to sing the "police brutality" line. They only need one person to say "chokehold." Consider what they had to work with: two teenagers --one who admits she's been using drugs for eight years, an immigrant whose English isn't good, a guy on probation for possession of drugs and a firearm, a lady who was gassing her car, and a store employee who went back inside while we're wrestling Owensby. You're about to read why only one of seven so-called witnesses testified at my trial. Aerial St. Clair was more or less the best of the worst. She only won the honor of being the state's "star witness" because she was willing to be led further by detectives than the others. Before we get to St. Clair, here's a sampling of statements the other "witnesses" gave:

--Katrina Peterson. Age 16. Peterson said: "He was attempt to run but they caught him. I couldn't hear anything. All I heard was when he's on the ground was "Mace the "

Q: "How many people were hitting him with a billy club?"

Peterson: "One. They hit him in lower rib, an upper ribs. About three times."

Q: "Did he comply?"

Peterson: "No."

Q.: "How many did it take to handcuff him?"

Peterson: "Well, it took nine or ten. Took about nine or ten ... Even Golf Manor an' them started jumpin' on him."

Q: "Did you see if he was maced?"

Peterson: "I don't think he maced him. He was just saying, 'mace him.'"

Q: "When you saw them run over to Sunoco, what did you do?"

Peterson: "I turn't around an' walked back like toward the phone booth, between Sunoco and Sam's."

--Juanita Rickerson, who was buying gas, said, "Subject walked out of Sunoco and he was met with two police officers. And the two grabbed 'im with black uniforms on ... Two of 'em commenced beating him."

--Saber Ayyad. Owner of Sunoco, said, "My partner told me police standing in the door. I jump from behind the counter and I see three officers talking to this guy.

Then he tried to run away from them. One of the officers jumped on top of him. After that I don't know what happened. I went back in the store. They pull him up. They took him to the police car. We couldn't come close to see what's going on."

George Weaver. A 20-year-old on probation for possession of 10 pounds of marijuana and carrying a concealed weapon. He starts off the interview saying there was "about 20 officers" at Sam's, just standing around.

Q: "What did you see the Golf Manor cops do?"

Weaver: "Right. Short, white, stocky."

Q: "Bald, stocky white Golf Manor."

Weaver: "Right."

Q: "Cop."

Weaver: "Right. That's the one that choked him."

Q: "He choked him? What about the other Golf Manor - I thought you said before that he hit him in the face."

Weaver: "The short blonde hair cop choked him. The short blonde hair cop that's the one that hit him in the face. That's what had his nose bleedin'."

Q: "That's not what you told us the first time. First time you said he choked him with his arm crossed around his neck."

Weaver: "The first time. I had it mixed up."

Q: "What were they telling him?"

Weaver: "Stand up. Stand on your feet."

Q: "I mean do you think somebody would be yelling at somebody to stand up and walk, if they knew he was unconscious? Does that make sense?"

Weaver: "Yeah, it makes sense ... But I'm not saying that's what really happened for sure. I'm just saying that's what I think happened."

Aerial St. Clair. She was 17 at the time of the interview.

Q: "How do you know L.A.?"

St. Clair: "L.A. Not hang with 'im. But like we be chillin' an' stuff like that."

Q: "What do you buy from him?"

St. Clair: "Marijuana."

Q: "Is it known that Mr. Owensby sells marijuana?"

St. Clair: "Yeah."

Q: "Were police being belligerent?"

St. Clair: "Oh, no not at all ... They came up to him normal. When they came up to him normal after that, he tried to run from 'em. But they caught him and then they tried to slam 'im in the ground. But he hit George (Weaver's) car then hit the ground. And they was trying to handcuff him but they couldn't."

Q: "Did Mr. Owensby comply, or did he continue to resist?"

St. Clair: "He continued to resist."

Q: "Severe struggle?"

St. Clair: "Yeah. He was trying to get away."

She says it took five or six police officers to handcuff him and she saw a police officer hit him with a club, in the lower back, "when Owensby was kicking at 'em ... Other police were punchin' him." According to her, he did not walk to the car.

Q: "When they slid him into the rear of the car. Does he appear to be conscious?"

St. Clair: "To me he did."

41

Q: "Now you said before, you just said here that he was hitting him with a stick when he was handcuffed. And you said before he was hitting him with a stick when he wasn't handcuffed. Now you're changing your story."

Second interview. Nov. 12, 2000

St. Clair: "From the time he hit the ground, that's how quick, that's how quick it happened like."

Q: "Did you hear what the police were saying?"

St. Clair: "Put your hands behind your back."

Q: "Was 'L.A.' doing what they said?"

St. Clair: "No... But then they got his right arm behind his back and they couldn't get his left arm. I really couldn't see his head. They was around him ... They got his left arm and then they was handcuffing' him. An' one officer was macing him. And then the other officer got on his, put his knee in his back and just started choking him."

Q: "So he had his knee on his back. And then he, you're indicating he had his, one of his arms."

St. Clair: "Uh-huh."

Q: "Around his neck."

St. Clair: "Yes, sir."

Q: "And choking him."

St. Clair: "Yes, sir."

Q: "And at what point, what was the position of 'L.A.'? Was both hands handcuffed at this time, or was he still resisting?"

St. Clair: "The officer, it's like as he was putting other handcuff on he was putting his knee in his back an' choking him."

Q: "Did he have the handcuffs on?"

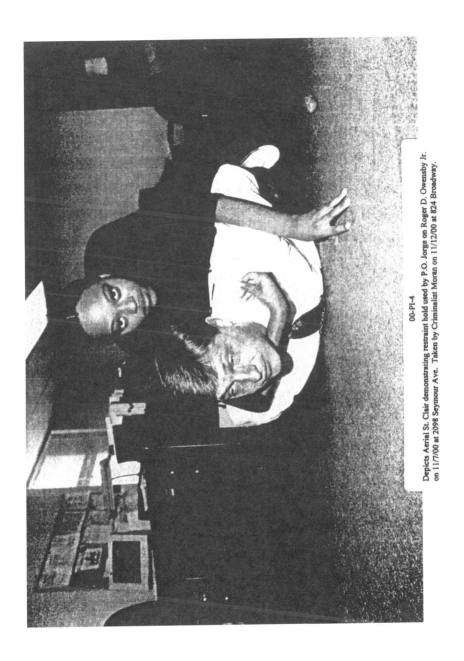

00-Pl-4

Depicts Aerial St. Clair demonstrating restraint hold used by P.O. Jorge on Roger D. Owensby Jr. on 11/7/00 at 2098 Seymour Ave. Taken by Criminalist Moran on 11/12/00 at 824 Broadway.

43

St. Clair: "Yeah, I guess he was choking him."

Q: "Okay, And how long do you th ... indicate, before we went on tape you basically went over this same story. Is that correct?"

Q: "We are trying to determine how long he had his arm around his neck. Is that correct?"

St. Clair: "A. Yes sir."

Q: "Approximate time. .."

St. Clair: "I don't know nothin' about stuff like that."

Q: "How long did you feel he was, you, we asked you how long you felt this lasted and timed it. And it came out to roughly ten seconds. Is that correct?"

St. Clair: "'L.A.' was still moving, but you could tell he was in pain ... just hearing him moaning. They just started dragging 'im to the car."

Q: "But this is before he had the, he went around and put his arm around his neck. I mean you're looking like you're confused and maybe I am confusing you."

St. Clair: "Yeah. I am."

Q: "Lineup No. 4 -you picked out No. 5. And you felt this is the officer that was the one kneeling on 'L.A.'s' back and then eventually put his arm around his neck?"

St. Clair: "Yes I do."

Q: "And you said that this is the officer that was doing this is the one that cut his sleeve off?"

St. Clair: "I seen 'im after he had took his, cut his shirt." Note: I was No. 3 in the line-up, not No. 5

Q: "Aerial, I want to go back over these. I'm showing you lineup No. 1 that I showed you prior to going on tape. Is that correct? And in this lineup you picked out ..."

St. Clair: "No. 2"

Q: "You said you saw this officer at the scene ... but he was involved in the fight ... You don't recognize anybody else being involved ... in this lineup?"

St. Clair: "That's correct."

Q: Lineup No. 3, you selected No. 2.... And you said you didn't recognize anybody else in this lineup ... In lineup No. 4, you picked out picture No. 5... And you felt this is one that you saw with his shirt ripped."

St. Clair: "And the one that choked him."

Q: "Okay, We're going to start the tape again."

St. Clair: "I just felt they drug him to police car. I think they already knew he was gone. But I think ... didn't wanna tell nobody."

Notice that St. Clair said nothing about a chokehold in her first statement. It's not until the second interview that detectives persuade her to go along with Dr. Parrott in saying there was a chokehold. I can imagine them telling her she can be a hero if she says she saw a chokehold.. . a conversation that took place while the tape recorder was off, no doubt.

St. Clair continued saying, "The officer, it's like as he was putting other handcuff on he was putting his knee in his back an' choking him."

Never mind that she repeatedly failed to pick me out of the two photo line-ups they showed her. Never mind that I would have had to have three arms to be able to do what she was saying.

Repeatedly turning the tape recorder on and off during interviews with St. Clair and Weaver, homicide investigators had no integrity. They were doing and saying things they didn't want on tape, and obviously felt no obligation to get to the truth. These men ended my career and nearly ruined my life. These people cheapened their profession.

To think I was indicted, tried, and vilified on the words of people like Weaver and St. Clair. It's criminal that Weaver was allowed to swear to observing things that he physically couldn't have seen, things he only "thought" he saw. But the grand jury had no way of knowing Weaver was inside the store while the struggle and handcuffing took place outside of his view. Leaders of the black community paraded Weaver in front of the press as an honest man, portraying him as the man who saw me choke Owensby. This man who changed his story has a history of drug arrests, and weapons violations. And we still don't know which detective gave the coroners office bad information about how long the struggle took. We don't know who mentioned a chokehold. We don't know why the coroner wouldn't tell the public that the theory didn't match the condition of the body.

As November neared its end, my wife and I traveled to Cleveland for Thanksgiving. When her family was arriving, I was reading the Cleveland Plain Dealer when I saw that there was an article about me. The pain and hurt I was feeling almost ruined my holiday. I talked with my mother-in-law about what was going on back in Cincinnati. While we were sitting in the basement, she helped me understand that God never gives us any more than we can handle. I truly thank God for that.

Chapter 6
Power of the Press

The media had no trouble finding a high-profile person to criticize the investigation of city police officers. No one wanted to be left out of the biggest story in Cincinnati for years. City councilman Todd Portune accused City Manager John Shirey of admitting that the Police Division was trying to cover up the facts surrounding Owensby's death. The council then voted for the appointment of a special prosecutor and demanded a grand jury investigation immediately.

Newspaper editorials criticized some council members, along with the police department for lack of information. The conclusion: The city manager must make sure investigations are handled thoroughly and impartially, and he must ensure Cincinnati's citizens are protected by the police force --not killed by officers.

Statements like that were disturbing, to say the least. No one had been indicted, no one charged, yet the media continued calling the deaths of Roger Owensby and Jeffrey Irons murder.

The daily dose of rhetoric by grandstanding politicians was interrupted by newspaper stories that purported to shed new light on use of force by Cincinnati police officers. In one article, a new --and unnamed --witness claimed, "All the cops were on top of him and he was screaming like crazy. Then they handcuffed him and choked him with a stick." According to this anonymous witness, police then pulled Owensby up, an officer stuck his baton down between Owensby's handcuffed hands and back, and then the police officers half walked, half dragged Owensby to the patrol car.

I shouldn't have been surprised that the media would publish such a sensational account and not identify the source. Such journalism is irresponsible, at best; criminal, at worst. But I was getting used to sloppy, sensational, and inaccurate reporting. It's obvious that the press plays an important role in our daily lives. But you may not realize how influential the press can be... until your name is the one in headlines.

January 12, 2001

To: The City and County Leaders

Re: Leadership, or lack thereof

Dear Ladies and Gentlemen:

I address this letter with respect to Mayor Luken, members of City Council, the City Manager, and Mike Allen and all the powers that be. At first there were tears, then numbness, followed by disbelief. I watched this ugly situation play, then the anger and now my own outrage. The City Fathers and Mothers went to the funerals of two men who choose to resist arrest and as a result of their own actions they escalated an arrest into a violent struggle and as a result lost their lives. The City leaders cried with the relatives of these men and they forgot about Officer Pappas who nearly lost his own life and threw away Officer Jorg like yesterdays bath water.

Officer Blaine Jorg was cut to the heart. He was stripped of his dignity, humiliated in public and left to be further vilified. When in fact he is a Police Officer of the highest moral character. A man who goes on duty with the hope that he can truly help someone. Not just to do what is necessary, but to actually make a difference in a positive manner. You have pronounced him guilty and not even bothered to look him in the eye, for if you did you would see an innocent man looking back at you. What a shameful demonstration of law and order.

Blaine has more integrity, honesty and value for human life than all of you added together.

Respectfully,

Joyce A. Jorg

Mother of Blaine Jorg, resident of Delhi, for I am ashamed to say that I live within the City of Cincinnati.

I'm not condemning all reporters. There are good reporters who make sure they get their facts straight. That was the case the first time I recall my name appearing in print, in September, 2000, when I was a volunteer at the Butler County Peace Officer Academy. It was an article by Jamie Morse, "Officer's Death Brings Home to Recruits." The article referred to the death of Officer Kevin Crayon. The reporter wrote, "At the end of the reenactment outside New Miami Elementary School Officer Jorg told the recruits that he knew Officer Crayon, then bit his lips together and swiftly turned and walked away."

I remember that moment well. A cop did his job, and he's not going home after his shift. Officer Crayon wasn't condemned for taking necessary action. That was fair and accurate reporting to Enquirer readers.

I was naive to believe every reporter would be as accurate. I soon found out that too many reporters knowingly report what they know is not accurate. They do so with immunity because few people complain. Well, I'm complaining. The press should be held accountable to high standards. Members of the press should play by the rules. The rest of us have to. If we choose to ignore the rules, we get penalized.

For the media, getting some of the story right most of the time seems to be the accepted standard. When you and I are misrepresented or maligned, we're told we can clarify matters with a letter to the editor. They can lie on the front page in big, bold headlines and we get to respond--days or weeks later --with a letter to the editor buried deep inside the paper. That's if they run a rebuttal at all. There's always a chance the letter will be heavily edited or won't see the light of day.

In my case, I can't begin to count all the errors that were reported by the media, particularly Cincinnati's two newspapers, The Post and The Enquirer. The first press accounts were full of inaccuracies, distortions and outright lies. Unfortunately, many of the errors were repeated time after time and were surely accepted as fact by the public. I'm convinced that these distortions in the press influenced the people who had the power to decide whether or not I would continue wearing the badge I had worked so hard to earn.

I won't bore you with every inaccuracy in every story, but how many errors were made in the very first article after Roger Owensby, Jr. died are frustrating to me. Note the glaring discrepancies in the November 8, 2000 Post article, "Man dies in police custody" by Jennifer Edwards:

--... Owensby resisted arrest, so two officers sprayed him with a chemical irritant."

--"When the chemical irritant did not subdue him, police called for additional officers."

-- "Witnesses said Owensby was flipped upside down, slammed onto the ground head first and reportedly punched by police after he was handcuffed."

-- "K. Johnson 20, who was at the convenience store buying juice, she said there were two officers in a car and they saw the man in the parking lot of Sam's, they yelled out for him to stop. "

--"Johnson said the man, whose street name is 'L. A.' ran into the adjacent parking lot. As the officers gave chase and closed in behind him, the man turned around "like he was going to give up.""

--'The two officers each took one of his arms,' Johnson said, 'handcuffed him, then flipped the man upside down and slammed him onto the ground head first.'

--'Then they started punching him all over. He was face down on the ground in handcuffs. Then he didn't make any sounds,' Johnson said."

--Johnson said there were two cameras hanging near the gas station front door.

Sure, some of these errors might seem minor, but they can't be shrugged off, especially when those errors paint a picture of police brutality. This reporter was loose with the facts and was irresponsible to quote any unnamed sources. The damage that resulted from this reporting was multiplied by the radio stations and TV stations that collect their news directly from the printed pages. This version of that night was spread far and wide, and it was eventually picked up by the national news, as well. I could only imagine what the Owensby family must have thought after reading that news article. I wonder if the coroner, Dr. Parrott, was influenced by these erroneous reports as he tried to determine why Roger Owensby, Jr. died.

Naturally, my family and I were quite upset by the errors in Edwards' article, so much so that my father voiced our concerns to Post Managing Editor Barry Horstman. When we discussed Edwards' article with Horstman he said: "I have seen, in other instances, what reporters are told on the scene or in the first hours afterward, weeks, months later, when more thoughtful reflection is brought to bear on the circumstances, those initial details don't always stand up. But they certainly weren't picked out of thin air. Jennifer Edwards' story represents what officers at the scene were telling her: This is what happened."

But Edwards did not interview any officers. The result is an article filled with untruths that's read by tens of thousands of people. In the rush to get the story and sell papers, no one bothered to get collaboration to make sure the story was accurate.

No wonder the community was frustrated and angry. The press fed them tales of rogue cops beating up an unarmed black male. Readers had no way of knowing the stories were based on inaccurate statements. The Post dealt another devastating blow to my reputation and showed further disregard for fact-checking in the November 9, 2000, story: "Tape shows beginning of fatal arrest-Owensby death may be strangulation."

On the previous day, Coroner Dr. Parrott reported that Owensby died of mechanical asphyxiation. But Dr. Parrott based his conclusion on three pieces of bad information: first, that there was vomit at the scene of the struggle; second, that the struggle lasted "two to three minutes"; and third, that an officer had applied a chokehold. I fully understand the newsworthiness of Dr. Parrott announcing that Owensby died of mechanical asphyxiation. Big news story, I know. But once again, the Post refused to allow the facts to get in the way of a sensational story:

--"As Owensby waited in line to pay for his purchase, an officer appeared-outside the doorway, baton in hand. ..As Owensby turned around to exit the store, the officer quickly tucked the baton under his left arm."

--By then a second officer, David Hunter joined the two (Owensby and myself).

"The witness said the five officers tackled Owensby."

--"All the cops were on top of him," the witness said... "They handcuffed him and choked him with the stick."

--"All (officers) have less than four years on the force. "

Thirteen false or inaccurate statements in two articles! And that's just the Post reporters. But other mistakes did irreversible damage, particularly statements from unnamed "witnesses" who say they saw multiple officers on top of Owensby, and at least one choking him. I couldn't help but feel like a target on the first day of hunting season. Reporters had access to first-hand evidence yet distorted the facts to sell newspapers. What angers me the most is that there's no accountability. When we presented the 13 errors and asked for explanations from Horstman and Post editor Mike Phillips, we were stonewalled.

The Enquirer followed suit. In the November 8 edition, reporter Jane Prendergast also quoted "K. Johnson." When asked if Johnson was male or female, Prendergast said she could not remember! Did she interview Johnson, or just lift quotes from the Post story? With such distortions being presented as facts, it's no wonder the NAACP and other African-American groups called for a U.S. Justice Department investigation on November 11 and organized plans for a protest rally at City Hall the Sunday after the incident.

Television news reports took the sensationalism the rest of the way. That night, they were saying we picked him up and slammed him head first on the ground, and that we took him behind a building and beat him, then came back around front and he was dead.

On and on it went. It reached the point where I couldn't read the papers, couldn't watch the news, because no one was getting it right. Reporters made hundreds of mistakes. Ninety-nine times out of one hundred, the reporter didn't look beyond the surface of the issues. Reporters almost always went for the sensational, even when it could be easily established that the sensational wasn't true. But the truth wasn't sexy enough; it wouldn't boost ratings.

In my trial, it was easily proved that what the media reported was wrong. The cameramen sat there and videotaped all of the witnesses coming in, all of the cops. And ninety-nine percent of the time the gist of what the officers said was, "He was a good cop. Never did anything wrong." But did they air comments like that? No, they didn't.

The inference is that I killed a man with a chokehold. News reporters totally ignored Sergeant Watts' comments about my character and professionalism. Viewers probably came away thinking this sergeant on TV is condemning a renegade cop, which isn't the case at all. The reporter sitting in that courtroom knew that particular sound bite doesn't truly represent the sergeant's testimony.

Watts knew from first-hand experience that I was a good cop. He rode with me one day because a drug dealer filed a complaint that I was harassing him. And I said, "Sarge, if you have a problem with what I do, come ride with me. Grab your bags, let's go." It took us about eight minutes to get to my beat, and after about two minutes of driving around I see a car without a front license plate. The driver wasn't wearing a seatbelt. So I turn around and follow him. I hit my lights. A short pursuit ensued. When he stops he tries to bail out. I grab him, take him to the ground, and with little resistance we cuff him up. Upon running the suspect's driving information, we find out that he is driving on a suspended license. I searched his vehicle after his arrest and I find crack cocaine on the driver side floor by the pedals. I look at the Sergeant --who's a black guy --and I say, "Sir, did I racially stereotype him?" And he says, "Blaine, I'm never riding with you again, you make me work too much." Sergeant Watts helped me with the paperwork, he helped me with the processing. He did everything. He said, "Blaine I don't have a problem with what you do."

The media reported what they wanted to report. Unfortunately, if they had a good investigative reporter they could have retrieved some real good information. Kimball Perry of the Post (who has since moved to the Enquirer) was one of the worst offenders. In his Oct. 24, 2001, article, he reports, "A Cincinnati Police Officer demonstrated how Officer Robert "Blaine" Jorg used his left arm to cover Roger Owensby's mouth and nose before Owensby died during his arrest November 7.

According to Perry, Officer Dave Hunter covered the mouth and nose of a mannequin during the reenactment, but that's not what happened. A TV news crew taped the demonstration and aired the footage that night. At no time did Hunter cover the mannequin's nose or mouth. In the same article, Mr. Perry reported that officers confronted Owensby in the store.

Early on, reporters at both the Post and Enquirer displayed a penchant for misrepresenting the facts and presenting unsubstantial hearsay as fact. They got St. Clair's age wrong. They were wrong about my length of time on the job, and the amount of money the Legal Defense Fund raised. Over and over again, they published inaccuracies, half-truths and outright lies. Their reporting was far from fair and accurate.

It's also worth noting what wasn't reported. On the video from the convenience store, at least seven other customers and a clerk are visible on tape. The media didn't report that at least seven people did not witness any wrongdoing by any policeman. Of course, there was no wrongdoing to witness.

There are only two television news people I trust. One is Clyde Gray, WCPO Channel 9 News, in Cincinnati. I used to attend every police graduation at the convention center. At one ceremony, two of the other officers I graduated with and I are sitting there when Clyde Gray comes walking down the aisle by himself. My buddy, Ron, stands up and said, "Hey Clyde, sit down with us." Well, now that we've put him on the spot, the only thing he can do is sit down next to us. So he comes down and we introduce ourselves. Clyde says, "So what's everybody going to think if you're sitting with the enemy?"

"Oh, we don't care, man. How are you doing?" Well, the event hadn't started yet, so we're sitting there cracking jokes, just having fun. At one point, we look over and he's got his head between his hands and he's crying, he's laughing so hard. When the ceremony starts we become professionals. After it's over, we start cracking on Clyde, because he was crying. We're trying to hand him a tissue, "See you next graduation."

"All right guys." He responds.

Sure enough, next graduation comes up, and we're sitting in the same place. He sees us, and his head goes up.

"Hi, boys." He comes over and sits down.

Three or four graduation ceremonies in a row, he sat next to us. Never got personal, never got beyond the hellos and how have you been. He joked, "If you make me cry this time, I'm getting up and walking out."

When Owensby died, reporters started hounding my parents because my dad's name and phone number were in the phone book. My dad called me and said, 'Channel 5 wants to come here and do a thing with me about you."

I said, "No, don't do it."

Channel 12 called. "No, don't do it."

Channel 19? "No. But if you get Clyde Gray from Channel 9, do it."

Well, Sam Louis from Channel 9 calls and says, "Hey, I met your son before." Which he did.

By now, dad knew what to say: "No, I don't want to talk to you, but if you send Clyde Gray out, I'll talk to him."

When Clyde came out, the first thing he wanted to know was why we chose him. My dad told him the story. And right then, he said, "Oh God, I know those guys. Okay, now I understand. That was your son. That guy is a nut case. How did he end up in this?' And Clyde did a very good job reporting the facts. He treated me very well. He treated me as a human being.

The only other reporter I trust is Julie O'Neill, also of WCPO Channel 9. She interviewed me, and it was the only time I said anything about the incident on camera. She also treated me fairly. I knew she would. I always watched channel 9 and I saw the work she did. I respected her. When I was contacted about the interview, I met her first and went over what could be talked about. She was straight forward, and caring. Today, six years later, I would be cautious with talking to most local TV reporter except Clyde Gray or Julie O'Neill--and one radio host, Bill Cunningham, WLW AM-700.

I feel I would have to be cautious with the newspaper reporters as well. Kristina Graves from the Enquirer came to my parents' house and interviewed my family. From that day on, it seemed like every two weeks she was on my front porch because she found out where I lived. She just started hounding me.

"The courts are deciding this on your future today, how do you feel?"

"I have no comment."

She was relentless. I told her at one point, "If you come on my property one more time, I'm advising you now you are not welcome. I'll be forced to call the police."

It's high time we as a society review the inadequacies of the press and demanded the media adhere to the standards of fair and accurate reporting they claim to treasure and uphold but routinely discard to sell papers, gain listeners and boost ratings. During the months since November 7, 2000, I have been repeatedly asked why I didn't give the facts directly to the press. The short answer is: "I don't trust most of them."

The reports about the Owensby case were so slanted, so incomplete, that I couldn't trust the media. How could anyone objectively review the press coverage of the Owensby incident and conclude that the police officers involved received fair treatment?

Chapter 7

Guilty Until Proven Innocent

The grand jury considering testimony against Pat Caton and I probably never heard anything about what kind of cops we were. We certainly couldn't tell them. Neither one of us was called to appear. Still, I needed an attorney, a good one. Scott Croswell came highly recommended, but he wasn't my first choice. A couple of police officers I knew of had used attorney Merlin Shivendecker, who is one of the best trial attorneys in Cincinnati. So I called Shivendecker and asked if he would be interested in representing me?

He said, "No." He was representing Pat Caton. Shivendecker said, "Let me call another guy and see if he's interested in taking your case."

I eventually contacted Croswell after I made some inquiries. Every single person I asked said, "If I ever had to go to trial and needed an attorney, he is the one I would choose, because he's very thorough, very good, and has a way with juries."

I was told he knew the law and was very good on his feet in court. When we spoke on the telephone for the first time, Croswell told me that he read and listened to some of the news accounts. He added that he hoped when I walked into his office I would be of slender build and one hundred-forty pounds.

When my parents met with Croswell in December, 2000, the word on the street was I would probably be indicted. This was confirmed when the Prosecutor's office called and offered a deal. Croswell was told the prosecutor would work with me if I would hang my partner.

Imagine that. They had decided someone was going to be the fall guy; it was just a question of whether it was me or Pat.

They also said that without my cooperation, there was a ninety-percent chance I would be indicted.

I shouldn't have been surprised that the prosecution and Croswell were discussing a deal. Especially after Croswell made a point to state that he knew

"Tommy" (Police Chief Tom Streicher), the coroner, (Dr. Carl Parrott, Jr.), and, of course, the attorneys at the prosecutor's office. He knew all the players, and he knew them well. I realized how well my attorney knew some of the men who held my fate when Croswell advised me that he was godfather to the son of Tom Langano, one of Allen's prosecutors. In fact, they lived in the same neighborhood in Clermont County.

Was I concerned that my attorney was the godfather of one of the guys trying to put me away? No. An attorney of Croswell's stature could keep his professional and private life separate, I believed.

I vividly recall Croswell sitting in his office, drawing a line down the middle of a page and saying, "This is what they've got. This is all the evidence we have that refutes it."

I looked at it, and I could only think, "How in the hell are they going to indict me?" They didn't have anything.

Then lo and behold, a couple of days later, Croswell says, "They're going to indict you. They have to, and I don't understand why, but they have to." I was trying to figure out what changed. I felt I was about to explode. When I left that meeting I slowly walked to my truck. I couldn't make heads or tails of this.

Sitting in Croswell's office another afternoon, I asked him point-blank, "What do you think is going to happen?"

He told me flat out that I was going to be indicted. I remember leaving his office in tears, walking down Sycamore Street to my car. I realized that I was probably going to end up going to jail for doing nothing wrong.

On January 4, 2001, I left Croswell's office and drove over to meet with Chief Streicher. I wanted to personally tell the chief that I made a good arrest, followed the book, and did not violate any police policy or commit any criminal act in arresting Owensby. Talking to the Chief was just something I felt the need to do. I wanted to tell him face-to-face. I was sitting outside the chief's office, knowing an announcement was forthcoming from the prosecutor's office, when I received a call on my cell phone. It was Croswell. He said it was imperative that I leave immediately and come directly to his office. The announcement of the indictment had been made and he did not want me to be arrested, handcuffed and led out of police headquarters.

At Croswell's office, I learned of my two-count indictment: 1. Assault, which is a misdemeanor, and carries six months if I'm found guilty; 2. Involuntary manslaughter, a felony that could mean five years in prison. "Pat was also indicted, he was charged with assault. I never felt so low in all my life. Everything I worked for was going up in smoke.

How could this be happening? I knew the prosecutors did not have any valid evidence. What would happen to Kristen if I go to prison? Where is the justice? I kept thinking to myself "Where are the rules and morals I grew up with? Where is God?"

My attorney and I went to the courthouse, two blocks away, and I turned myself in. I actually filled out my own booking sheet. I was then taken to the processing section. It was then and there that I suffered the humiliation of being fingerprinted and having my mug shot taken. I was put in line with prisoners, people I had arrested. They knew me, and they all looked at me, with a bizarre expression, "What the hell is he doing here?" It was one of the most humiliating days of my life. I thought, "If it's true that what doesn't kill you will make you stronger, I'm going to be Hercules when I come out of this."

News of the indictment spread quickly. By the time I left the courthouse, a number of uniformed and plain-clothes police officers were waiting for me outside as a show of support. That was the lone bright spot of an otherwise terrible experience.

Back at my attorney's office, Croswell's said he would defend me for $250 per hour, or a flat fee of $50,000, with a cap of $75,000. I guess I hadn't real-ized how much it would cost to prove my innocence, not until that moment. Of course, I didn't have anywhere near $50,000, but I knew my dad would exhaust his savings--and then some--if that's what it took to see that justice was done. What choice did we have?

I remember my dad saying, "Fine, $50,000."

He also said that he would be responsible for payment.

Croswell asked, "How do you intend to pay me?"

Dad responded, "$10,000 a month." Dad then asked Mr. Croswell to put the fee agreement in writing. I was in shock and disbelief as I left Croswell's office. I felt like I was trapped in a nightmare.

My attorney began earning his $50,000 at my arraignment, which I did not attend. I was in no condition to expose myself to the cameras and questions of the media. It's impossible to live with all the false allegations and hotheads boiling over with hatred. Not one of them knew the facts. I was called a murderer, a racial predator, and even accused of planting false evidence. All I could do to survive was pray and draw on the support from family and friends.

Some good news came our way after Croswell and his investigator, Greg Hensley, met with two attorneys from the prosecutor's office and a member of the coroner's office. According to Hensley, the coroner's office could not prove there was a chokehold. In addition, there was not sufficient time for officers to kill Owensby by piling on top of him. "Great," I thought. "So the case will be thrown out the window."

The Post was the first newspaper to report the indictment. They reported that, "In a chokehold, an officer wraps an arm around someone's throat." It was a big story: Blaine Jorg, the first Cincinnati police officer in 213 years to be indicted for a death in custody case in Cincinnati. Norma Holt Davis, president of the local NAACP chapter, said the group applauded the indictments but questioned why only two officers were indicted.

Reverend Damon Lynch urged a boycott of downtown businesses in protest of Owensby's death and alleged racial profiling. William Kirkland, a spokesman for Special Forces of the Black United Front, called the whole process a scam. John Heibling, attorney for the Owensby family, said Roger Owensby died because the officers had too little experience.

My attorney was quoted as saying, "(Jorg) believes the charges that have been brought are improper and there's no basis for them and he will be vindicated...(Jorg) adamantly denies that he violated police standards in apprehending Mr. Owensby. My client is as affected by the tragedy in Mr. Owensby's life as anyone. He views it as a tragedy that anyone would die under that set of circumstances. It's pretty heavy for someone who does not even have a disciplinary write-up in his file. He's astonished by the whole thing."

Keith Fangman, Fraternal Order of Police, President, had even stronger words. He reminded everyone, These officers are innocent until proven guilty." He then told officers to "think twice" before making some arrests. "It's not worth losing your job, your family and your freedom to try to restrain someone in that split second because you don't know the rules of engagement," Fangman said.

He put into bold words what officers had been whispering among themselves. If something goes wrong in that split second, will we be charged with assault? Fangman and the FOP were beautiful. I can't say enough about the support I received. Right away, on January 4, the FOP established a legal defense fund for me and Pat, who had been charged with assault. The fund turned out to be very successful, raising over $75,000 for our combined legal defense. The response by law-abiding citizens, fellow police officers, and fire organizations was unbelievably compassionate.

A part of that fund came fellow officers, friends and supporters who held a number of fundraisers. They were well attended. People from the neighborhood we worked in came. We even received contributions and encouragement from members of the prosecutor's office who attended FOP fundraisers. City Council members also contributed money, but asked that their donations remain confidential. Some senior police officers did the same thing. "Here's money (for the fund), but don't tell anyone." I understood their silence. Siding with Jorg and Caton wasn't something a city employee could advertise, although the county auditor didn't seem to care what anyone thought when he attended one of the fundraisers.

Not everyone approved of the legal defense fund. Rudolph Owensby, Owensby's grandfather was quoted in the newspaper, "It's really a race thing. It don't make me angry. It's what they do."

Scott Greenwood, a lawyer with the American Civil Liberties Union of Ohio, said the fund was "divisive and unnecessary." Fangman responded, "Greenwood's opinion means nothing to us. The ACLU constantly crows about their support for the First Amendment right to free speech. Obviously, he doesn't believe that applies to police officers."

The FOP was the only politically involved Cincinnati-based entity willing to be visible. Media-wise, radio talk show host Bill Cunningham was the only person speaking out against the indictment. Cunningham did more than talk; he was the first one to donate to the fund, with a $500 personal check. On occasion, a police officer I had trained would show up and spend some time with me. Support from those officers cannot be measured.

I received over three hundred cards and letters of support, most from people I had never met. One elderly lady sent $10 with a note that if her electric bill was not too high next month, she would send in another $10, just like the widow's mite.

What really moved me was the hundreds of telephone calls, and police officers of all ranks stopping at my house to check on me, showing up with pizza, and discussing everything under the sun but the case itself. They knew I had to get my mind onto something else. Cincinnati has a large number of professional people wearing the blue uniform. My dad says most of the officers he saw at the house were black. I hadn't noticed that.

When the grand jury indicted me, Chief Streicher said that Pat and I would remain on paid administrative leave while the case went to trial. He also promised citizens that all the facts would come out at the trial. Back then, I felt that Chief Streicher was behind me. That feeling didn't last very long. By the time I left my pay hearing with the city's Assistant Safety Director on January 4, I knew the Chief had abandoned me.

When we arrived for the hearing and were exiting the car, my attorney looked at me and said, "Let me tell you something I firmly believe now: You're either one hundred percent innocent, or the most evil man I've ever met."

I asked Croswell to explain himself.

He said, "You're either one hundred percent innocent, or you committed cold-blooded murder for absolutely no reason, left absolutely no physical marks on this man's body, then convinced five cops to cover it up without saying a word. In my mind, that's evil." At that point I knew he believed me.

Mr. and Mrs. Owensby were waiting for me at City Hall. Along with about two hundred other people there to show me support. Owensby's mother said she wanted to see the man who killed her son. Of course, the press reported that comment. They did not, however, publish the words of my wife, Kristen, who told Mrs. Owensby, "If you look my husband in the eye, you will see an innocent man."

Fangman was outraged at the results of the hearing, telling the press, "The city has declared war against our police officers... This prevents Jorg from getting funds from his retirement and deferred compensation accounts to live on and pay for his defense ... The decision today should send a clear message to every police officer in this city and their families and our supporters, that this city, this administration has declared war against their very own police." Fangman also said, "Pay can't be taken away from the officers, because nobody proved they have done anything wrong... To take away an officer's pay is a form of discipline. How can you discipline these officers when they've not been found guilty of anything?" Fangman promised to file a grievance to get my pay reinstated. He did, but the proceedings were delayed for months.

When Mayor Luken insisted that morale was very good, and there was, "... no war or vendetta against the Cincinnati Police Department," Fangman responded, "we don't put a whole lot of stock in what Mayor Luken says on this issue. This is the same mayor who called for a special prosecutor... Inflamed the issue, before he even knew any of the facts of the case."

So there I was, suspended without pay, but still under the policies and procedures of the City of Cincinnati, which state that if I want to work anywhere else, I have to put in a request and have it approved. I put in for an outside work permit to teach at the police academy in Butler County. Five months later Col. Janke turned down my request to teach. He put "DENIED" at the bottom of the form, crossed out the approval of 2 other command staff members, signed it, and sent it to me. Of course, I told officers that Janke did this. Later I was told that Janke went to every single police district and told them that I never put in a work permit. He said, "Blaine's lying." The cops were not sure who to believe. They couldn't believe that Jenke would do that. When I showed them my request form, with the "DENIED, Janke" they were stunned.

The whole thing got me wondering. Why would the department suspend me without pay when the city did not have one shred of evidence of any wrongdoing? The only answer I could come up with is that I was being pressured to quit.

A week after the indictment, the pressure increased. Assistant Safety Director, S. Gregory Baker announced, "There will be charges brought for violations of police division policies." He didn't say what policies I had violated, but he said that the range of discipline could be anything from counseling to termination. I had been stripped of my police powers, had my pay taken away and now there was talk of internal charges being brought against me.

CINCINNATI POLICE DIVISION
OUTSIDE EMPLOYMENT WORK PERMIT

EMPLOYER# _____

R. BLAINE JORG	P285 DIST4
EMPLOYEE	BADGE DIST/UNIT SOCIAL SECURITY #
D. RUSSEL LEE POLICE ACADEMY	3603 HAMILTON-MIDDLETOWN RD. HAM. OH
NAME OF OUTSIDE EMPLOYER	EMPLOYER ADDRESS
ROGER HOPKINS	868-6300 30004923-0
CONTACT PERSON AT BUSINESS	PHONE # WORKER'S COMP. #
TRAINING AT THE POLICE ACADEMY	VARIOUS AREAS IN THE TRI-COUNTY AREA
TYPE OF BUSINESS OR SERVICE OFFERED	ADDRESS WHERE EMPLOYEE WILL WORK
	$18.00/HR HOURS PER WEEK VARIOUS
DETAIL COORDINATOR (IF PRIVATE DETAIL)	RATE OF PAY YOU WILL WORK

DETAIL WORK SCHEDULE: VARIOUS HOURS AS SCHEDULED BY ACADEMY COMMANDER. NOT

TO CONFLICT WITH DIVISION HOURS.

PERMANENT x☒	TEMPORARY ☐	PERMIT ☐	12 /01 /00	/ /
PERMIT	PERMIT	RENEWAL	STARTING DATE	ENDING DATE

☐ SELF EMPLOYED   ☐ UNIFORM - POLICE SERVICES
☐ OWNER   ☐ NONUNIFORM - POLICE SERVICES
☐ PART OWNER   ☒ PRIVATE EMPLOYMENT, POLICE RELATED
☒x NONE OF THE ABOVE   ☐ PRIVATE EMPLOYMENT, NOT POLICE RELATED

EXPLAIN THE SPECIFIC DUTIES YOU WILL PERFORM: INSTRUCT AT POLICE ACADEMY
WHICH HAS VARIOUS LOCATIONS IN THE TRI-COUNTY AREA

I CERTIFY THE ABOVE INFORMATION IS TRUE. ALL OUTSIDE WORK WILL BE DONE OFF DUTY AND NOT CONFLICT
WITH CITY EMPLOYMENT. I UNDERSTAND IF I'M INJURED OR KILLED WHILE EMPLOYED IN THIS CAPACITY, MY
BENEFITS AS AN EMPLOYEE OF THE POLICE DIVISION ARE LIMITED TO THOSE AREAS OF EMPLOYMENT CONSIDERED
AS POLICE RELATED SERVICES. THE OTHER AREAS OF EMPLOYMENT ARE LIMITED TO THE WORKER'S COMPENSATION
LAWS OF THE STATE. I FULLY UNDERSTAND SECTION 3.4, 1.(e)(1) OF PERSONNEL POLICIES AND PROCEDURES
WHICH STATES: SICKNESS OR INJURY CAUSED BY OUTSIDE EMPLOYMENT CANNOT BE CHARGED TO SWP.

_____ P285 _____ 11 , 7 , 00
SIGNATURE OF EMPLOYEE   DATE

THE UNDERSIGNED REVIEWED THE ABOVE APPLICATION FOR OUTSIDE EMPLOYMENT. AS WRITTEN, IT DOES NOT
INTERFERE WITH THE EMPLOYEE'S POLICE DIVISION WORK, INVOLVE A CONFLICT OF INTEREST, OR PROVIDE AN
IMPROPER SERVICE TO THE OUTSIDE EMPLOYER.

_____   _____
DISTRICT/SECTION COMMANDER   EMPLOYEE'S BUREAU COMMANDER

_____   _____
AFFECTED DISTRICT COMMANDER (if applicable)   POLICE CHIEF

_____
DETAIL COORDINATION UNIT

DATE PERMIT CANCELLED AT DETAIL COORDINATION UNIT: ____ / ____ / ____

3/14 Denied

FORM 668
(REV. 7/94)

City Of Cincinnati
Notice of Disciplinary Action, Layoff or Displacement

Social Sec. No. [| | | 1 | 3 | 3 | 0 | 0]   Name _Robert B. Jorg_

Address _4150 Reading Road_

City,State,Zip _Cincinnati, Ohio   45229_

Job Title/Classification _Police Officer_   Dept./Div. _Safety/Police_

This is your Notice of: ___X___ Disciplinary Action
(Check One)

_____ Layoff

Effective Date
of Disciplinary
Action, Layoff, [0 | 1 | 2 | 5 | 0 | 1]
or Displacement

_____ Displacement to position of _____

Complete For All Disciplinary Actions

Reason Codes (Enter up to 3 codes)			Penalty Codes (Enter up to 2 codes)		Hours Penalized (Enter if applicable)
1	2	3	1	2	Indefinite/Indictment
0 7			0 1		

01—Failed Probation
02—Incompetency
03—Inefficiency
04—Dishonesty
05—Insubordination
06—Neglect of Duty
07—Failure of Good Behavior
08—Substance Abuse
09—Excessive Absenteeism
10—Violation of C.S. Rules/
   C.S. Law/Code of Ethics
11—Other

01—Suspension W/O Pay
02—Loss of Vacation Time
03—Loss of Off-Day Time
04—Loss of Holiday Time
05—Demotion*
06—Reduction in Pay*
07—Dismissal*
09—Other

*Personnel Action Form
(Form 14) required

Complete For All
Layoffs and Displacements
Reason Codes
(Enter 1 Code)

_____ _____

41—Lack of Work*
42—Lack of Funds*
43—Job Abolishment*
49—Other

*Personnel Action Form
(Form 14) required

Specifications: Attach a sheet giving full details of the charges so that the employee may be placed fairly upon his/her defense. Include disciplinary action(s) assessed, including dates and nature of offense(s), except written reprimands older than three (3) years. If demotion/displacement in lieu of layoff, include new title. If Job Abolishment, include one of the following reasons: 1. Reasons of Economy 2. Lack of Work, or 3. Reorganization for the efficient operation of the employing unit.

_____
(Appointing Authority)

This Notice Served Upon:
Robert L Jorg
By Registered Mail/Certified Mail/ Personally (Strike out those not applicable)

This __25__ Day _JANUARY_

_2001_ At _3 40_ O'Clock __P__ M.

Cinmy Ksm
(Signature of Individual Service This Notice) _Capt. (Mary) KSm-lu_

11S #0024B/TT
1 White—Employee 2 Canary—Civil Service 3 Pink—Department 4 Goldenrod—Division

To The Employee:

You have 10 calendar days from the date this notice is filed with the Civil Service Commission in which to appeal this action to the Civil Service Commission. Dismissals, demotions, layoffs, displacements, reductions in pay, suspensions of more than 3 days (uniform police personnel may appeal suspension of any duration) and first half probationary failures are appealable.

(Appeals must contain the person's name, address and phone number and be sent or brought to Room 215, City Hall.)

Approved As To Form By Law Dept.:	Dept./Div. Head Initials:
Approved As To Equity By Personnel Dept.:	

66

Chapter 8

"Enough is Enough"

"Officer Shoots, Kills Suspect" screamed a headline in the April 8, 2001 Enquirer. It was another opportunity for the press to make people look sideways at the police. The article detailed how Cincinnati Police Officer Steve Roach shot and killed Timothy Thomas, an unarmed nineteen year-old shortly after 2 a.m. Thomas, who was wanted on fourteen warrants --most for failure to appear on various misdemeanors and traffic charges--died at 3:02 a.m. on April 8.

I won't review all the information pertaining to the Roach/Thomas case, but I will comment on some parallels to my case, especially since my name came up when the shooting occurred, just as it does every time there's an allegation of police brutality.

After the Thomas shooting, riots broke out in the city, accompanied by the expected posturing by elected officials and others prominent in the community. Just as it had in my case, the media did its part to misinform, inflame passions, and fail to present both sides of the story. Cries for "justice" echoed throughout the city before the ink was dry on the Enquirer pages that told how Over-the-Rhine residents were concerned about police brutality.

No one bothered to point out that the tragedy could have been avoided if Thomas would have been responsible enough to appear in court and take care of his traffic warrants, and had not led police on a late-night foot pursuit.

The shooting increased already stressed relations between the embattled Cincinnati Police Division and the citizens who found themselves again demanding answers. Patience was wearing thin. On April 9, protestors carrying signs with messages like, "Enough is Enough," and "Prison Time for Officer Jorg," packed City Hall chambers. Thomas' mother said, "We deserve to know why." Initially, Roach said that he shot Thomas because he saw a gun as Thomas moved his hands to his waist. One could reasonably ask, "What would I have done under those circumstances if I were in Officer Roach's shoes?"

Myself? I don't know.

Politicians and leaders of the black community didn't waste any time demanding sweeping change and reform within the Cincinnati police department. They kept repeating a common theme: fifteen shootings of black men by police in the six years since 1995. No one mentioned that none of the fifteen deaths were murder. No one said, "We could have had fifteen police funerals." No one pointed out that in ten of the fifteen instances, the victim shot at police or aimed guns at officers. In the other five incidents: One suspect used a knife, one used a brick against policeman, another swung a board with rusty nails embedded it. Two used cars as weapons.

Fangman was on the money when he said that Cincinnati police officers are not some band of rogue Nazis roaming city streets hunting down and killing black men. But time and time again, the reporting is inflammatory, it's racist, and it's wrong. People continue to assign race to issues of violence. It is believed by some people, that only white police officers fire their weapons. That's not the case.

Three of the last four shootings were by black police officers. It doesn't matter what race a suspect is, if a suspect acts in violent manner, as a cop you fear for your life, you will revert to your training and take necessary actions to defend yourself and protect citizens.

What happened to Cincinnati was not a black-and-white issue. Twelve of the last fifteen police officers murdered in the line of duty were killed by black males. Since eighty percent of the cops murdered were killed by black males, is it fair to say all black males want to kill cops? Of course not. That would be racist, inflammatory, and unfair. It's just as wrong to say all white police officers want to murder black males.

A television analyst asked why no whites had been killed by Cincinnati police since 1995. Here's the answer: there were several shot but didn't die, for example a person who wielded a sword at officers. He was shot multiple times; however he did not die from his injuries. When that happened I don't recall one protest demonstration being organized. In Cincinnati, eighty percent of the murders are black on black, 15 percent are black on white, and five percent are committed by whites or others.

Yet it is rare to see protests against drug dealers or black-on-black crime. Black leaders seldom discuss this topic. Someday the leaders of the black community will learn that the police are not the enemy. Unfortunately, this wouldn't happen in time to help me, Pat or officer Roach.

Instead, Council Woman Minette Cooper wails about, "A fundamental problem with the police division." Reverend Lynch announces at a City Hall meeting, "We are not leaving until we get answers." Vice Mayor Alicia Reese calls for a special meeting of council to be held at the convention center. There is a call to select future police chiefs from outside the city. Mayor Luken then adds, "Too many blacks are being killed at the hands of the police." With this sensational, but ridiculous statement, Mayor Luken lit a short fuse of an angry community.

Amid the unrest, the grand jury for officer Roach is empanelled. Eeveryone knew there would be an indictment. Commenting on Fox TV'S Hannity & Colmes program, Sergeant Steve Rogers of the national support group AmeriCop said, "Justice by intimidation, the grand jury members were intimidated... if the grand jury does not render a verdict to their liking, see your city burn." I believe he had it figured out.

It was obvious that my trial, scheduled for May 10, 2001, would be delayed. That meant my opportunity to prove my innocence--already on hold for five months--would have to wait. My new trial date was set for October 22, 2001.

Indictment or not, the protests turned violent. Rioters, mostly youth, destroyed businesses downtown--not for justice, but for fun and profit. Twenty-eight windows at City Hall were broken. As the violence spread down Race, Findley, Liberty and Vine streets, more businesses become targets of thrown rocks, bottles and looters. Schools are closed, as was Music Hall. Dozens of properties were damaged and looted. One white truck driver from Louisville is pulled out of his truck and beaten by a group of about 20 protesters just because he is white. Police were in riot gear, and when necessary, fired bean bags and rubber bullets.

Mayor Luken called a news conference to appeal to the city for calm. After mentioning that the situation is "very fluid," he warned, "... the police are ready if violence continues." He also says, "the young people are taking advantage of the situation." He later says to Bill Cunningham that, in retrospect, his comment about too many blacks being killed at the hands of police was not good.

Still, the rioting continues. Local news stations tell people to stay away from downtown. Reverend Lynch remarks, "We know they are going to set fires tonight. The kids told us what they were going to burn." Sure enough, fires were set.

With fires raging in the Findley Market area, gunshots and roving bands of rioters kept things tense all night. One policeman was shot, the bullet hitting his belt buckle. White people's cars were rocked, and even black businesses were damaged and looted. Bottles were thrown at police.

It was a full-scale riot. Cincinnati was a city under siege, and anything was fair game: metal pipes, bricks, baseball bats, anything. Businesses continued to close and board up windows. One black girl told a TV reporter, "We can't let police keep killing us, it's bad enough we are doing it to ourselves." Bean bags fired by the police hit children, old men and a pregnant woman. Some people claim the police are acting like cowboys.

If people stepped back and looked at the problem objectively, they'd realize the cops were just trying to control the crowds for public safety, and for the safety of officers. But there wasn't much objectivity in the days following the shooting.

So Mayor Luken held another news conference to reassure citizens that his administration was taking every precaution to keep the violence from spreading. He announced that he had contacted black leaders and did not plan to request outside help from the National Guard. He wanted to make more information available to the Thomas family.

By now, the networks were all over the story. ABC News reported that the FBI was looking into the situation. Mayor Luken admitted that the, "City (is) deeply divided along racial lines." His only answer to the violence was handcuffs and tear gas. Of course, there is a lot of anger and frustration aimed at the police. In two days of civil unrest there were one hundred -fifty arrests. One individual who was interviewed said, "It is not an East-West problem, not a black-and-white problem, but North versus South in the most historical sense."

Cincinnati all but shut down. Finally, the Mayor set up a mandatory curfew.

Throughout the unrest, the new Black Panther Party, Malik Saabazz, Rev. Al Sharpton, and others get headlines promoting their own agendas. All of these people explained that the cops are the bad guys. One of the black leaders says, "This is not a riot, but a rebellion." The local NAACP and Baptist ministers take a more sensible approach, saying there are many ways to address the problems other than violence. With the eyes of the nation watching, Mayor Luken, Ohio Governor Bob Taft and Ohio Secretary of State Ken Blackwell attended the funeral of Timothy Thomas, which was followed by a peaceful march.

Police remained under fire. There was still a lot of anger. Some people complained about what they called "unequal enforcement", that patrols were heavier in black neighborhoods than white ones. Never mind that common sense dictates placing your resources where the problems are, not on quiet streets miles away. On that Saturday there were two hundred-twelve arrests, mostly curfew violations. Police officers were working twelve-hour shifts. Days off had been canceled.

My wife and I were in California at my sister's house for Easter. We were afraid to come home.

Allen says in the news, his office will provide evidence to the grand jury. He adds that the presentation will be, "... very thorough and fair. We must leave no doubt about the process." I don't recall Allen promising to be fair and thorough in the presentation of the evidence to the grand jury when I was indicted. But he could afford to say that this time.

According to the news reports, prior to deliberations, prosecutors told the grand jury, "There is no public purpose to be served in indicting a person when it appears that the evidence is insufficient to sustain conviction, and unjust and unfounded accusations should not be made against anyone."

I have to ask, "Were the same instructions given to jurors when I was indicted?" Allen came away from the Thomas grand jury proceedings saying, "We must treat the results of this case as any other. In this atmosphere we must leave no doubt about the process."

That's a pretty dramatic departure from what he said when the Owensby grand jury presented its findings: "When you arrest someone, you can't kill them, it's that simple."

Allen had learned from the mistakes his department had made in my case. Officer Roach was found not guilty without having to endure the stress and pain of a jury trial. Hamilton County Municipal Judge Ralph E. Winkler exonerated Officer Roach, saying, "The shooting was a split-second reaction to a very dangerous situation created by Timothy Thomas. That, under all facts and circumstances heard at trial, was a reasonable reaction on the part of Officer Roach."

Chapter 9
Argue the Truth

There was a lot of back-and-forth going on between my attorney and I as we prepared for the trial. The first thing he told me do was write out a detailed statement of what occurred. Then we reviewed every witness statement that was given to the homicide unit and picked them apart, piece by piece. We narrowed down a list of witnesses we wanted to call, and tried to determine who the prosecution would use. Then we listed what experts we had, including doctors and self defense experts.

Looking at everything, I felt the strongest thing we had was the truth, the fact that I didn't cause Roger Owensby's death. Croswell, on the other hand wanted to argue I killed him, "but this is why."

I told him, "No. I didn't do anything wrong."

He responded, "So, we'll argue the truth."

Croswell never discussed any problems he thought we would have. We went over everything multiple times. It became monotonous and tiresome. I hated even thinking about going to Croswell's office. However, I learned everything about the case that was going to be brought against me.

A lot of questions were raised in the defense camp, and waiting for the trial to answer those questions was agonizing. The tension and fear I was under was excruciating. I could hardly eat anymore, and I couldn't sleep. I cut myself off from my wife and my friends. I wanted to be left alone. If I didn't have to go to my attorney's office, I would have just as well preferred to call him from home. As my trial date approached, I had some mixed feelings about Croswell, but I still trusted him.

Kristen's parents came in town from Michigan about a week before the trial. The morning of the trial my parents, Kristen and her parents, and my closest friend, Brian, gathered at our house. I asked everyone else who was coming to meet us at the courthouse. I was on overload. Before we left, we held hands in a circle and prayed.

ACTION - RESPONSE
USE OF FORCE CONTINUUM

IMPORTANT - The list of officer responses is *not* intended to be in any specific order, but reflects on the amount of resistance encountered. The officer will choose the necessary response to gain control of the situation based on departmental policy, his physical capabilities, perception, training and experience.

OFFICER - SUBJECT FACTORS

1. Age
2. Sex
3. Size
4. Skill Level
5. Multiple Subjects/Officers
6. Relative Strength

SPECIAL CIRCUMSTANCES

1. Closeness of a Weapon
2. Injury, or Exhaustion
3. Being on the Ground
4. Distance From the Subject
5. Special Knowledge
6. Availability of Other Options

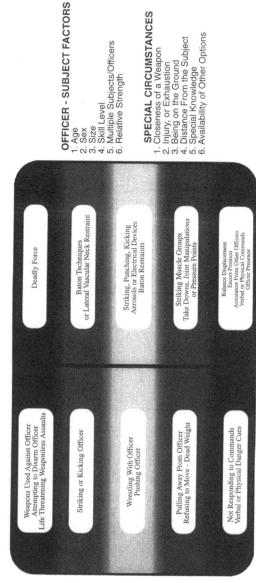

INDIVIDUAL'S ACTIONS	OFFICER'S RESPONSES
Weapons Used Against Officer / Attempting to Disarm Officer / Life Threatening Weaponless Assaults	Deadly Force
Striking or Kicking Officer	Baton Techniques or Lateral Vascular Neck Restraint
Wrestling With Officer / Pushing Officer	Striking, Punching, Kicking / Aerosols or Electrical Devices / Baton Restraints
Pulling Away From Officer / Refusing to Move - Dead Weight	Striking Muscle Groups / Take Downs, Joint Manipulations or Pressure Points
Not Responding to Commands / Verbal or Physical Danger Cues	Balance Displacement / Escort Position / Assistance From Other Officers / Verbal or Physical Commands / Officer Presence

Continuum of Arrest: Control – Handcuff – Search – Evaluate – Transport

The press seemed to be everywhere as Kristen and I met Croswell and our families entered the courtroom. Everyone wanted a sound byte, but we were silent. Inside the courtroom, there was a still photographer from the Enquirer and a news camera from a local TV station. Croswell and I were told by the judge's clerk that Court TV wanted to carry the trial live. Fortunately the judge agreed with a joint motion and barred them. It was way out of hand. The judge had ruled that each cameraman would share footage and photos with their competitors. Television monitors were set up in the hallway outside the courtroom for television reporters covering the trial. My family and newspaper reporters sat behind me and Croswell. The Owensby family, their lawyer, and their friends sat on the other side of the aisle.

I was under a great amount of stress. The courtroom was full of people who loved and believed in me, but I still felt alone and stressed out. With no paycheck since being suspended in January, I couldn't help wondering what the future held. But, I mostly felt disbelief that I was even on trial. I couldn't help feeling I was a character in some bizarre play. I was a sacrificial lamb being led to slaughter.

As I waited for jury selection to begin, I glanced over at the TV camera. The media had already created considerable damage with lies, distorted facts, and unnamed sources. My attorney was talking with the judge, my family was amongst themselves, and I was sitting by myself. I felt as if I was on display.

When my attorney walked back to our table, I glanced over my shoulder. I saw my wife looking at me, there was a peace about her, I felt somewhat comforted by her look. Croswell sat down next to me and it began.

Jury selection went fast. Croswell didn't dismiss one prospective juror. During instructions to the jurors, Judge Nurre said his "guesstimate" was that the trial would take about two weeks, but that it could take longer. What a depressing thought. I hoped he had overestimated how long I would have to make it through this.

One of the prosecutors, Longano, laid out the state's case, that A) Roger Owensby was taken into custody by Cincinnati Police and the defendant is Robert Blaine Jorg; B) and the allegations that the State of Ohio has brought against him is that as a result of certain things that took place during the arrest, Roger Owensby died in custody of the police.

Longano added that, "The State of Ohio alleges that the Cincinnati police officer used excessive force during the arrest of Roger Owensby, which caused his death." I learned they would only call one civilian witness, Aerial St. Clair. In addition they would call two doctors and the father of the deceased. It had been eleven months since the incident, and they only had one civilian witness even though there must have been twelve to fifteen others at the scene of the struggle that night.

Around 4 p.m., the counsels had selected a jury of twelve ladies and gentlemen and alternates, who were asked to stand and receive their oath. Then the Judge read the charges. Count number one: The defendant is charged with involuntary manslaughter. The elements of the charge are: one, on or about November 7, 2000, in Hamilton County, Ohio, the defendant caused the death of Roger Owensby as a proximate result of said defendant committing or attempting to commit assault. Count number two: The defendant is charged with assault... the defendant knowingly caused or attempted to cause physical harm to Roger Owensby."

By this point I was numb, literally. I couldn't feel my legs, and my stomach was in knots. I don't remember much from the rest of the day. But it finally ended. Somehow, I was supposed to eat something and get a good night's rest.

As I lay awake that night, I hoped that no law-abiding citizen ever ended up in the same position I faced. At least I had the love and support of a great family. Not everyone has that. But that night, I needed my space. Thankfully, they understood.

Croswell had one thing right. After the jury was sworn in, he told me, "The case has just been decided." In short, regardless of the prosecution's case -despite their witnesses and evidence and despite our facts-the jury had already decided the case. What a scary and unfortunate thing.

Tomorrow, the trial would begin with jurors visiting the Sunoco lot. And then, the prosecution would start calling witnesses.

I had entered a plea of "not guilty". I would finally see Ariel St. Clair. I had never met her, but I had seen pictures of her demonstrating the alleged chokehold. In the photos, she had her right knee in the small of a man's back, her right forearm across his throat, her left hand on the ground. And she said I was handcuffing Owensby at the same time. I couldn't wait to hear what she would say in court. I thought about St. Clair's conflicting statements, and how no two people seemed to witness the same thing.

In my head I kept hearing two things. One was Croswell's voice saying, "Blaine, how did you ever get indicted?"

The other was a friend of mine who saw Mike Allen at a social function and Allen told him, "I wont loose any sleep if Blaine doesn't get convicted."

I lay on the bed staring at the ceiling as a streetlight outside cast a slight shadow into my room. I said a short prayer that the truth would be made known to everyone, that a clear picture would be taken from this horrible event.

Chapter 10
A Genuine Tragedy

The trial began on Tuesday, October 23, 2001, just two weeks shy of a year from the night Roger Owensby, Jr. died. A jury would finally decide who was telling the truth: Aerial St. Clair was key. She was the only person they could persuade to say that I choked Roger Owensby. But on the eve of the trial, St. Clair appeared less than convinced that she saw an officer choke the guy she bought drugs from. She told Channel 19 WXIX, "Well, I was watching it, and it all could have been an accident."

As Tom Longano began opening remarks, I felt very much alone. I knew the support was there, but I was the one on trial. Longano told jurors he would call several witnesses to support his key witness, Aerial St. Clair. Her friend, Katrina Peterson, would be called. So would Ted Schoch, an instructor from the police academy; Sabil Ayyad, an employee at Sam's Sunoco; and Joan Burke, who works for Hamilton County Coroners office in the serology department.

I knew the whole case hinged on Aerial St. Clair. In his opening statements, prosecuting attorney Mark Piepmeier said, "Jorg went too far, and he crossed the line that officers aren't allowed to cross... He was reckless, and his reckless act caused serious physical harm to Roger Owensby, which ultimately caused his death." Croswell countered by saying, "At no time did my client or any other Cincinnati police officer that I'm aware of, choke Mr. Owensby. At no time did my client in any fashion inhibit Mr. Owensby's ability to breathe."

With opening statements out of the way, the prosecution led off with Roger Owensby, Sr., who explained that his son had been a cook in the U.S. Army, in Bosnia. I guess Owensby Sr.'s testimony was intended to establish his son's character, that his son was a defender of freedom, not a drug dealer.

Sergeant Anthony Carter, who headed up the investigation, was the prosecution's next witness. When asked whether a "chokehold" was permitted by department policy, Carter said, "Use of a chokehold is illegal, improper and unethical... It would be excessive use of force. It is not necessary."

It made for a good television sound byte, but Carter never said that I used a chokehold, or excessive force. That's because I never did.

During cross-examination, Carter admitted that there was no vomit found at the struggle scene. That's important because the lungs usually discharge fluids when asphyxiation occurs. When my attorney asked, "What did you find at the struggle scene?" Sgt. Carter evasively answered, "I don't remember. I would have to refer to my notes."

Croswell shrewdly said, "Where are your notes?"

Carter answered, "At the office." So my attorney said, "We'll wait here until you have it. Go get it." So they sent another detective back to Homicide. He came back, and Carter got back on the stand. My attorney had him read his notes. No vomit at fight scene, no blood, either. Just like that, my attorney shot down all the press headlines.

Croswell, knowing how badly the prosecution needed to prove that Owensby died at the scene of the struggle, finished by having Sergeant Carter admit there were no scuff marks consistent with being dragged on the toe area of Owensby's shoes. The inference: it wasn't an unresponsive, lifeless man officers dragged to the police car; the man was walking.

I didn't think Carter's testimony was the command performance prosecution attorneys hoped for. Longano had plenty of damage to undo with his star witness, Aerial St. Clair.

When asked why she was in court, Aerial replied, "They kept coming to my house." Then St. Clair painted a picture of police brutality, saying that after officers climbed off Owensby's limp body, "I thought he was dead right there." She also demonstrated how I supposedly put my arm around Owensby's neck while I had a knee in his back.

It was a compelling testimony for spectators and reporters, but St. Clair got more wrong than right.

St. Clair claimed that officers went into the store that night to get Owensby. On the witness stand, she testified that she did not see the macing; she only heard the command to mace Owensby. St. Clair couldn't even state her correct age. On the stand, she said she was 19. She was 18.

I remember thinking, "How long will I have to sit here before I can tell the truth and let the Owensbys and all the others know what actually happened? I have kept silent for nearly 10 months, and now I must remain silent while they lie to my face."

It was eating me up because what I was hearing from the witness stand was not the truth. I was prepared to testify and take the witness stand. I kept thinking about my nephew, Kevin, asking his mom, "Why is Uncle Blaine on TV. so much?"

On Wednesday, the prosecution opened with Officer Hunter, the one who started the whole chain of events by telling Pat and I that a man walking across the street appeared to be a guy who assaulted him a few weeks earlier. To this day, I don't know how Hunter could have identified the man from one hundred twenty-five yards away on a poorly lit street. Pat told me later, "There is no way he could have identified him from that distance in the dark. There's no way."

Using a mannequin, Hunter demonstrated how I "lay" on Owensby's side and controlled his head. Hunter testified, that I told him I learned the head restraint at the police academy. He pointed out that officers are forbidden from attacking suspects' heads unless deadly force is needed to protect an officer, or others.

When he was questioned by Croswell, Hunter admitted he never saw me place Owensby in a chokehold, and didn't see me do anything criminal during the incident. But according to Hunter, Pat crossed the line. Hunter claimed Pat jumped on Owensby's back and punched Owensby, "numerous times." He also said Pat was, "swinging" at Owensby while placing him in the cruiser, but he couldn't see if Pat actually struck Owensby.

When Croswell asked, "Was Caton acting crazy enough to do anything over there?"

Hunter replied, "I don't know." Then Croswell asked, "You don't know whether he choked Roger Owensby or not, do you?"

Hunter's answer: "I don't know."

Croswell asked Hunter why he didn't do anything if he thought Owensby was in medical despair, and why he was one of the officers "high-fiving" everybody if he thought the man was in trouble. Hunter wasn't able to answer. He was totally unprepared for a video from Officer Spellen's cruiser to come out that showed officers celebrating after Owensby's arrest.

The prosecution hoped to recover with a convincing testimony from Dr. Schultz, who performed the autopsy. His testimony would be crucial. Dr. Schultz emphatically stated that, "this gentleman absolutely did not move once he got in that police cruiser because he was dead."

I guess he didn't know that witnesses saw Owensby moving and heard him cursing as he was walked to the cruiser. Other witnesses described Owensby being in different positions when they observed him in the back seat of the police car. Croswell asked what it would mean if the vomit was found where Mr. Owensby was laid after he was removed from the cruiser. Dr. Schultz refused to acknowledge it would be a very significant finding. Croswell then informed Dr. Schultz that his ruling was based on inaccurate information because there absolutely was no vomit at the struggle scene.

Dr. Schultz continued to insist, "He didn't die in the police cruiser. He died when he was on the pavement." Croswell never got Dr. Schultz to admit that Owensby could have died some place other than where we struggled with him. Dr. Schultz was absolutely, one hundred percent correct when he testified, "...vomit came out of his mouth... people who die from asphyxia die from vomit all the time."

"I was told vomit was on the ground beneath him at the struggle scene," he testified. That, of course, contradicted what Sgt. Carter had said the day before, that the Homicide unit did not find any vomit at the struggle scene.

On the way home that day, I asked Kristen, "What do you think?"

She said, "Don't say anything." She knew the prosecution would twist something I said. I don't remember much about that evening. My friend Brian came to the house to keep me and my wife company. I remember sitting in my basement, watching the news cast about my trial. I was angry at how the media distorted the facts of the case. The way they televised the trial was so different from what actually took place. They showed a cut from Dr. Schultz saying that Owensby was dead on the ground. But, they didn't show Croswell during cross examination. Nor did they show Carter confirming that there was no vomit found at the struggle scene.

On Thursday, the prosecution tried to reinforce its case by calling other officers, and the coroner, Dr. Carl Parrott, to the stand. The prosecution began with Darren Sellers, one of the officers who walked Owensby to the Golf Manor police car. The counsel expected the officers to testify that I had used excessive force, or caused Owensby's death by kneeling on his back. Sellers came close to giving them what they wanted, saying that Owensby was unresponsive when he arrived on the scene. But then also he said that it was very difficult for us to handcuff Owensby.

Sellers wouldn't say that I had my knee in Owensby's back. Prosecutors asked, "Officer Jorg was up in this area?" Gesturing to the area between the shoulder blades.

Sellers replied, "He was here somewhere. But I don't remember if he was kneeling down or standing up. But I just know he was in the area."

Counsel then asked, "You weren't watching him?"

Sellers' replied, "No." Like Hunter, Sellers left the stand without giving the prosecution their chokehold.

The next witness, Golf Manor officer Robert Heiland, flatly contradicted Sellers' claim that Owensby was unresponsive when we walked him to the car. Heiland correctly pointed out that Owensby was struggling as officers put him in the cruiser. Then Officer Abe Lawson agreed that Owensby was alive after the handcuffing.

The final witness of the day, Sergeant Pete Watts, was better than any witness we could have called. In describing my character, Watts revealed that he conducted my annual evaluations, and he said I was, "the epitome of a well-rounded beat officer", and that I was always willing to share information with others. Watts also called me, "one of the best FTOs (field training officers) we have." He said that I should take the sergeant's test.

Watts was asked by the prosecution, "Have you ever seen Officer Jorg over-react?"

"No, I haven't." Was the Sergeant's response.

The prosecution then continued asking questions such as, "Have you ever seen Officer Jorg run into a situation he couldn't handle?" and the answer was no.

Watts admitted that he had received two complaints about me since I went to District Four, but then he explained both were unfounded. One, for excessive force, turned out to be another officer. The other complaint was an accusation that I was profiling some young kid. The office of municipal investigation ruled that the complaint was "completely unfounded."

Longano and Peipmeier turned to their medical "experts" to fill the gaping holes in their case. The prosecution wanted to establish that some of the fluid on the sleeve of my uniform, which I cut off because it was contaminated, had come from Owensby's lungs. Dr. Parrott was called to establish that Owensby must have expired on the ground where the struggle occurred, and that in doing so, he vomited up fluids because I had choked him. Interestingly, the prosecution never asked Dr. Parrott about a chokehold.

During the cross examination, Croswell proved that the prosecution was grasping for straws that simply were not there. Yes, there were fluids on my sleeve: Sweat, blood, chemical irritant and maybe saliva.

Croswell asked Dr. Parrott "Is there a scientific test that you can do for pulmonary edema?"

Parrott answered, "Not that I'm aware of."

Croswell continued with, "But what you have told us is there is no scientific test available to tell whether the pink stuff that you see here (on the shirt sleeve), in fact, is this substance that you say comes from the lungs, correct?"

Parrott answered "That's correct."

Croswell started to turn up the heat on the coroner, "But you're not telling us it's edema are you?"

Parrott shrugged, "To a scientific certainty, no." As for the infamous chokehold, the coroner could not say there was one, and he couldn't rule it out.

Croswell then asked "...to you as a coroner that this was some type of strangulation or you used the term 'mechanical asphyxiation.'"

Parrott replies, "Yes." Croswell asked him to explain with more clarification. Parrott continued, "Since we don't really know what happened. We can't really be certain exactly what happened at this point."

Fifty weeks after Owensby's death, and the medical experts still couldn't say how Owensby died. "At this point..." As if the coroner was expecting additional information to come out. Dr. Parrott defended himself by saying, "My autopsy doesn't point the finger at anybody. My autopsy tells me how he died--asphyxiation."

I waited for Croswell to totally discredit Dr. Parrott's findings, but my attorney let the coroner off the hook. Croswell had promised jurors that he intended to "sharply challenge" the coroner's findings, but instead he engaged in what felt like the shortest cross examination in history. Croswell never asked why the coroner's case report contained erroneous information that vomit was found where the struggle occurred. He never asked the coroner how he knew vomit was found where I wrestled with Owensby. In fact, Croswell never mention the word "vomit" to Dr. Parrott.

The prosecution's final witness was Cincinnati Police Officer Todd Brunner, who was called to show that the hold I used wasn't a technique taught at the police academy. Brunner really was an expert witness. For three-and-a-half years he'd been an instructor in defensive tactics and physical fitness. Brunner acknowledged that the mandibular angle pressure point hold I used to free Owensby's arm from under his body for handcuffing is absolutely permitted and completely within department guidelines. Brunner stated, "Utilization of the mandibular angle pressure point is within department standards when confronted with noncompliance suspects. The maneuver is reasonable when the duration is limited to that time required to gain the desired compliance."

The prosecution, still trying to recover, asked if that the type of hold Brunner explained would suffocate a person. Brunner replied, "No, it only causes pain." Brunner demonstrated on the mannequin how the mandibular pressure point is applied. During cross examination, Brunner pointed out that the courtroom was a very sterile environment, the mannequin was not fighting back, and the dynamics of such a hold changes dramatically in a real-life situation.

Early Friday afternoon, the prosecution rested. They had not called St. Clair's friend, Katrina Peterson, nor Sabil Ayyad, the man who worked at Sam's Sunoco. Longano had promised to call Joan Burke, who works for Hamilton County Coroner's office, and Schoch, the expert who appeared before the grand jury. Had Longano just been blowing smoke? Did they ever intend to put the other people on the stand?

They hadn't put on much of a case. Aerial St. Clair was the prosecution's only civilian witness who was allegedly at the scene. Her convoluted testimony raised as many questions as it answered, and should have had everyone wondering how close she actually was to the contact, pursuit, struggle, and handcuffing of Owensby. It wasn't the case the prosecution had promised to present during opening remarks.

That day, Croswell and I had a little sit-down in the back corner in the courthouse, and he asked me, "How do you think it's going?" I told him that they haven't proved anything. They are going around in circles. He replied, "Well, what do you want to do?"

I said, "What do you mean?" Do we put on a defense or do we not? That was where this conversation was going.

I said, "Scott, every witness we were going to call, the prosecution called, except the use-of-force expert and a doctor. The use-of-force expert the city used basically agreed with us. The doctor we totally blew out of the water. So let's not put on a defense." He agreed, but wanted to know if I wanted to take the stand and tell my side. I said, "I don't know. There are pros and cons."

He said, "You'll get up there and tell your side and they will try to sink your ship. So what do you want to do?"

I replied, "Can I let you know in the morning?"

He said, "Okay."

Kristen helped me make the right decision. She said, "What if you say one thing and it comes out another way?" That's what I was worried about. We didn't want that. Especially since we were winning anyway.

I wanted to take the stand and tell my side of the story, but there was no need. Croswell and I agreed that the prosecution had failed to prove the charges of involuntary manslaughter or assault. Did I make the right choice? They had the burden to prove their case and they failed. We didn't have to prove anything we just had to show where the holes were in their theory. So the next morning Croswell announced, "The defense rests."

While my trial was wrapping up, Pat's trial was in full swing. They started within a few days of each other and it wasn't a coincidence that they were going on at the same time. It was if they knew that information from one trial would disprove theories in the other.

The whole thing was just bizarre. In my case, the prosecutor argued that I killed Owensby on the ground. In Pat's case, the prosecutor claimed that Pat beat Owensby on the ground and while dragging him to the car, then beat him some more at the cruiser. Same incident, same Owensby, but in one trial he's dead at the scene of the struggle, and in another courtroom in the same building, he's alive after the struggle. It got crazier. In Pat's trial, Aerial St. Clair testified that she's never seen Pat Caton before. Pat was only one or two feet from me during the struggle, and she never saw him before! But I'm not surprised. After all, she repeatedly failed to identify me when detectives showed her photo lineups shortly after the incident. St. Clair also testified that she smokes marijuana daily and that she was "high" at the time of the incident.

Another thing that jumped out at me from Pat's trial was the testimony of Dr. Schultz, who said that he didn't see any injuries when he looked at Owensby's back, and that it was possible bruises cannot be seen. So why did the prosecution in my trial claim that I had caused bruises by putting my knee on Owensby's back?

I wish I could have paid closer attention to Pat's case, and supported him. It had been a grueling, exhausting, tension-filled week for me. For five days I did not go to lunch with my family, my friends, or my attorney. Sheriff's deputies found me an empty room, and I spent my lunch breaks there, alone. Thankfully, Brian was at my side all week. He was great. He parked the car, bought sandwiches, made telephone calls and lifted my spirits time after time. I would need his support more than ever on Monday when closing arguments began. And then would come the verdict.

Chapter 11
Closing Arguments

The case against me was becoming weak. I expected Longano and Peipmeier to compensate by coming on strong during closing arguments. I thought they would let it all hang out, pull out all the stops, and put on a really impressive show. Longano tried to portray me as an aggressor, but his attempts were pretty feeble. For instance, he said that at the beginning of the incident that my nightstick was out and I was "taking a stand." The convenience store video clearly shows me holstering my stick while Owensby is still in the store paying for his cigars and energy drink.

After portraying me as spoiling for a fight, then wailing on the suspect, Longano attacked my claim that I was attempting to protect Roger Owensby's head during the struggle.

"I think when you look at the evidence, it would fly in the face of common sense," Longano said. And, "You're not going to find any evidence that he was attempting to apply a pressure hold." Longano claimed that the head wrap I applied was contrary to the policies and procedures of the Cincinnati Police Department. That claim totally contradicted their witness, Officer Brunner, who acknowledged that the mandibular angle pressure point hold I used to free Owensby's arm from under his body is absolutely permitted.

Obviously, Longano didn't understand the benefit of a mandibular angle pressure point hold, or the necessity of freeing the arms using this technique. I wondered if the jurors understood any better than he did. About the strongest thing Longano said was, "Blaine Jorg was on top of him." Longano told jurors that a good test is to match up what a witness says to the physical facts that have been established beyond a reasonable doubt. I hoped they would think long and hard about these "physical facts".

Longano tried to give the impression that we had quite an ordinary situation: subject runs, wrestle him to the ground, and handcuff him. I wish it was that easy. I would love to place one handcuff on my wrist and ask Longano, Piepmeier or their boss, Mike Allen (a former policeman), to put the handcuff on my other wrist. They wouldn't be able to. But I'd be willing to let them try.

Longano asked jurors to weigh the testimony of the two doctors who alleged that mechanical asphyxiation was the cause of death. He referred to a grinding bruise, which he claimed is consistent with a knee in the back. He also mentioned petechia in the eyes--a condition that occurs when someone is deprived of oxygen--and the fluid in the lungs that Longano claimed ended up on my shirt sleeve. His conclusion: Roger Owensby, Jr. was dead on the ground. Longano quoted Officer Sellers as saying that when he arrived, Owensby wasn't moving. Longano didn't explain why Sellers would need to assist with handcuffing and escorting a dead man to the police cruiser.

In reviewing the testimony, Longano said that Sellers saw "Officer Jorg delivering some strikes, and he wasn't sure if it was with a fist or an open hand to the back of Roger Owensby's head..."

Sellers said no such thing. But what really burned me was when Longano said that the police officers either weren't paying attention during the incident--or they just didn't remember--but his star witness Aerial St. Clair did pay attention. Longano then contradicted himself. He admitted that she was wrong about which arm was around Owensby's neck, and then acknowledged she changed her story about how long the alleged chokehold lasted. First, she had said it lasted 10 seconds; later she said it was 2 minutes.

St. Clair was hardly an ideal witness. Longano even admitted it. He told jurors, that she "came to court with a little baggage." But Longano still insisted that St. Clair had told the truth, that her testimony should be believed above all others.

"To convict this man, you have to believe Aerial St. Clair is telling the truth, and you have to believe Officer Hunter is a liar when he comes in here and tells you that he observed the entire incident and Blaine Jorg did it by the book," Longano stated.

Longano stated that St. Clair based her testimony on the medical testimony, which established the facts. This eighteen year-old, who is a known drug addict, based her testimony on numerous visits from homicide detectives. It's preposterous to say she based her testimony on medical testimony.

Longano said some questionable things, but most of his closing argument was fairly tame. It definitely wasn't an all-out attack on me. In fact, Longano delivered his closing arguments in a soft voice, and with little conviction. I kept expecting him to say something like, "You must find Officer Jorg guilty." But he didn't. Instead, he told jurors that if they aren't convinced, "... you render a verdict of not guilty on each count."

Longano also told the jury, "There is no question about it, some witnesses lie. Some witnesses can testify to things that they perhaps saw that were distorted. But the physical facts don't lie." What a strange thing to say since every witness who took the stand was a prosecution witness. Remember, we didn't call a single defense witness. So in effect he was saying, "We know some of our witnesses lied and distorted the facts and are not always credible."

All in all, Longano didn't hurt me very badly. When he discussed the assault charge, same thing. "If we prove that Robert Jorg knowingly caused or attempted to cause physical harm to Roger Owensby, then we have made our charge of assault..."

The most noteworthy thing about Longano's summary is that he never mentioned the word chokehold. Not once. For nearly a year, the press had been reporting a chokehold. The coroner had said, "a chokehold, gone bad."

Longano had also said "positional asphyxia" could cause death in certain situations. But no one mentioned "positional asphyxia" during testimony. Where did the term come from? Why would Longano mention it in his closing remarks? The trial was a disgrace for the prosecution, and an insult to clear-thinking citizens. I faced a prison sentence courtesy of politicians, and coroner's office, homicide detectives, and police chief who wanted touse me to take the spotlight oof of them.

Croswell didn't come on as strong as I thought he should either, but he was clear with his argument. I appreciated him pointing to my exemplary reputation and calling me a professional officer, who at all times uses good judgment, one who is fair and respectful to everybody, whether black or white, poor or rich, whether you come from an advantaged background or disadvantaged background, whether you are mentally advantaged or mentally disadvantaged. Whatever it is, he treats everybody with respect." Croswell added, "He's a man who has received commendation after commendation from the police department and excellent reports."

He also mentioned that the department had never received a complaint of excessive force involving me.

Croswell also did a fantastic job of discrediting St. Clair. He said the most significant flaw in the prosecution's case was that St. Clair didn't mention a chokehold during her first interview with detectives, but on the witness stand testified, "I watched the man climb on his back and choke him to death with a cross-arm bar chokehold."

Croswell asked jurors, "Do any of you, as you stand here today, think Aerial St. Clair's testimony is believable beyond a reasonable doubt? Wouldn't she be screaming, 'Choke, choke, I saw them choke him,' when she gave her first interview?"

Croswell also attacked her claim that she observed the incident from inside the convenience store. He pointed out that on November 7, 2000, St. Clair told police she was inside the store and saw Pat and I enter, have a conversation with Owensby, and escort him outside. She said she followed Owensby out and watched everything. The video from the store shows that no officer entered the store. The video also showed St. Clair, long after the struggle and handcuffing, walking to the back of the store, not out the door. Croswell said, "... her testimony is totally, completely, absolutely 100 percent unworthy of belief." He also said, "I didn't present a defense because I'm not going to dignify what's been presented with a defense."

In reviewing Dr. Parrott's testimony, Croswell pointed out that a homicide does not necessarily mean that a criminal act caused the death. Besides, the coroner could not say that a chokehold had definitely occurred.

"And guess what? The prosecutor didn't even ask him (the coroner) if he could say it was a chokehold," Croswell said. "Didn't even ask, 'cause he knows he can't say it's a chokehold."

Croswell stated, "The prosecution has the burden of proof. When the coroner says it could be any of the three, then it's incumbent upon them to show that it's the choke, and not positional asphyxiation, and not piling on. Now, other officers said that he walked to the car, and two (officers) said, that he was moving in different positions in the car."

On the edema question, Croswell told the jury, "Dr. Parrott said, 'It looks like edema, but I can't tell you it is.' Did Dr. Parrott know Owensby was perspiring? He never went into that." Croswell asked if Dr. Parrott knew that I had my arm around the man's forehead so that Hunter could mace him.

"He didn't know that?" Crowell answered himself, "If you're laying flat on the ground and the liquid is in your lungs, is it going down towards the ground, or is it going to fall at a 90-degree angle out of your mouth? It's out of your mouth. You heard Mr. Longano say that. The bottom line is there ain't no way it can be edema under the facts and circumstances that you all heard."

"In the final analysis, the prosecution has to prove to you that Roger Owensby was choked to death by my client, Blaine Jorg," Croswell continued. "And I would suggest to you that they failed miserably and that all the evidence, the evidence presented by them, is contrary to that theory. All of it is contrary to that theory. The State has failed miserably to prove the case against my client. Each and every witness has testified favorably for my client, with the exception of Aerial St. Clair."

"The reason the state has failed miserably is through no fault of their own. They presented what they had. And the reason, ladies and gentlemen, that the facts failed miserably to convict my client is because, in fact he is innocent. He didn't do anything wrong, and that's why they can't prove that he did."

"I'll finish simply by saying that I have an absolute commitment to the proposition that the only reason that the prosecution failed miserably to prove their case is because there was no case to be proven in the first place. And my client, as he sits here today, is as innocent as he was one minute after the conflict. He's a decent man trying to do a decent job. And I personally think it's a damn shame he has to go through this trial."

Peipmeier wrapped things up for the State of Ohio. He began by apologizing for another final argument, and said it was his duty. He said, "We are not here to judge Officer Jorg for his entire career. And contrary to what Mr. Croswell said, we're not here to determine this case solely on the testimony of Aerial St. Clair." He mentions, you heard about the training the officers receive, what happens when they put out an 'officer needs assistance' call. And, they are allowed to use force when they make an arrest. But with all that comes a limit, a duty, and that's what this is about. Don't cross the line. We're saying that for a few minutes on November seventh, he was reckless, he crossed the line."

I bristled when Peipmeier called my conduct, "reckless". After admitting that there was no proof the fluid on my shirt-sleeve was edema, Peipmeier said, "Roger Owensby didn't just die. He died because somehow his oxygen was restricted... Who could have caused that? Which officer restricted his ability to breathe? We've got everybody pretty much excluded, except Officer Jorg. What did he do? Well, we can't be sure exactly what he did... He put aside his training, and he did something to cut off Roger Owensby's breath. It was reckless."

Peipmeier then shifted gears and attacked Pat, calling him "a bum", and saying that he should not be a cop. Why make such statements? Was he trying to deflect the spotlight from me to another cop at the scene?

In his charge to the jury, Judge Nurre explained that to find me guilty of involuntary manslaughter beyond a reasonable doubt, jurors had to believe I caused the death of Roger Owensby as, "a proximate result of committing or attempting to commit an assault." The judge also defined, "recklessness: A person is reckless when, with heedless indifference to the consequences, he purposely disregards a known risk that his conduct is likely to cause a certain result. Recklessly includes conduct that is knowingly or purposely performed."

The jury was dispatched to begin deliberations at 11:40 a.m. that day I could only hope they would base their verdict on fact, not hearsay and speculation. If they focused on the facts, I would soon be exonerated. The physical facts were clearly in my favor. For a while I replayed the trial in my head.

I had the situation under control that night. Roger Owensby, Jr. was cooperative as I questioned him. But his demeanor changed when Hunter stepped forward and said, "That's him. That's him." Did his demeanor change because he recognized Hunter? Could be. Hunter admitted to being a "friend" of the Owensby family. But why would Owensby run from a friend? Maybe Hunter was an enemy, not a friend.

After we handcuffed Owensby, as we started to go to the vehicle, Hunter stepped in front of me and took over my position. Darren Sellers was with Pat when they took Owensby. So when Hunter stepped in, I let him take the prisoner. By the time I grabbed all my equipment and headed back to help them at the car, the doors were shut and Owensby was inside.

The funny thing is that there were three or four officers who took Owensby to the car, but afterwards the only person who would admit to taking him to the car was Pat. But Pat wasn't the only officer involved. More than one cop said he saw two black officers putting Owensby into the car-the two black officers who took off as soon as they realized there was a medical need. As soon as sergeants started arriving, these two black officers went behind a building and talked. They returned three to five minutes later.

This is where the complexities of the situation arise. We had three witnesses --two civilians and one police officer--telling homicide detectives they saw Dave Hunter, "the small black officer," striking Owensby's forehead with his nightstick, in short, jabbing motions. Two civilians and one officer. And it was a black cop saying Hunter was hitting Owensby.

I never saw it. I can't say in a court of law that he did it. But three witnesses say he did it. Keep in mind, other cops were keeping the crowd back. I mean it only takes a second or two to hit a guy three times. If you're not right there when it happens, you're never going to see it.

The grand jury never heard that information. But if you look at the autopsy pictures, you see circular indentations and scars exactly matching the butt-end of a nightstick. You have statements that Dave Hunter hit Owensby with a nightstick, and you have physical evidence matching it, but no, that's never brought up, that's never mentioned.

I do know that Hunter is a bold-faced liar. At the trial, he said that once the handcuffing was over and everybody stood up, that Pat stayed on top of Owensby and was punching Owensby. That never happened. Pat has never done anything like that. Why did Hunter say he did? I don't know. Pat hit him, Dave maced him. I used a pressure-point hold. And the rest of the struggle consisted of officers using joint manipulation and pressure points in an effort to keep his hands in the same spot. That was it. Nothing that we hadn't been trained to do.

Those were some of my thoughts as I sat in the meeting room while jurors deliberated. But my main thought was: "At last, in a few hours I'll know the outcome. Do I go to prison or do I go home? And when I'm found not guilty, will I be able to continue in my chosen career as a police officer?"

My family was there, my brothers-in-law, and my friend, Brian. We waited, and waited, and waited some more. Croswell kept coming and going, each time telling us, "They haven't said anything yet."

At 2:35, jurors asked for a chalkboard and copies of the trial transcript. But the judge denied the requests, telling them to use their collective memories regarding what the witnesses said.

By 9 p.m., the jury still hadn't returned a verdict. They would try again in the morning. I wasn't unnerved that deliberations would extend into a second day. I remained confident. I knew I didn't commit a crime or break any department procedures. But I was a anxious.

The next day, Tuesday, it became obvious that jurors were having trouble understanding the issues involved. At 10:55 a.m., the jury reentered the courtroom to ask Judge Nurre if they had to convict me on the first count to get to the second count. The judge told them to return to their quarters and reconsider the issue that they didn't understand.

At 11:30, they returned and submitted their question in writing: "Based on the wording of Count one, are we deliberating on the verdict of Jorg based on: 1. He was the sole contributor to the death of Roger Owensby, or 2. He was one of several contributing factors to the death of Roger Owensby?"

After considerable discussion with counsel, the judge replied in writing: "In order to find the defendant guilty in Count one, you must find that but for the defendant's conduct, Roger Owensby would not have died, and you cannot hold the defendant responsible for the conduct of others." I probably took my first deep breath when I heard the question... and the response agreed to by the judge and the attorneys.

That afternoon, the Court was informed that the jury was deadlocked on Count one, but had reached a verdict on Count two. The judge instructed them to continue deliberating, despite an objection by Croswell. "Their message has been explicit that they have explored all options and are unable to reach a verdict," Croswell said "It is cause for me to believe that enough is enough. They have deliberated for fifteen hours ..."

Judge Nurre, unmoved by Croswell's plea, reminded jurors that, "It is your duty to decide the case, if you can conscientiously do so. It is conceivable that after a reasonable length of time honest differences of opinion on the evidence may prevent an agreement upon a verdict." If that occurred, the jurors were instructed to return to the courtroom.

The jurors returned at 6 p.m. to inform the judge that they were still dead-locked, unable to arrive at a unanimous decision. "Hearing the transcripts that we requested would still not get us to a unanimous decision," the foreman reported. He added, "In Count two we have reached a verdict."

Croswell came in and said, "Blaine, I've got good news and bad news. They have decided. They have a verdict on one charge, and they don't on the other."

I say, "Okay, what does that mean?"

He said, "From my point of view, they found you guilty on the assault, and they're hung on whether the assault actually killed him."

I said, "Okay."

And he said, "Let me find out more." And he left. So now I'm dealing with that. When he came back, he said, "They're ready for you."

I was sweating. I was freaking out. I called Brian and Croswell over, and I said, "Croswell, if they convict me on assault, am I going home tonight or are they locking me up?"

He said, "You'll still go home. I'll make sure of it."

I said, "Okay."

I told Brian that as soon as they read the verdict to get my truck and meet me at a certain location because, "We're getting the hell out of here."

As we walked into the courtroom, I grabbed Brian again and I said, "Whatever you do, keep an eye on Kristen. Make sure she's taken care of." I told my brothers-in-law the same thing. My mom couldn't stay in the courtroom. She sat through the whole trial, except for the verdict. She had to leave. She told me later that she couldn't stand to sit in that room. So she walked out to my dad's car and prayed the rosary. Back in the courtroom, more waiting. I thought the jury was already seated, but they hadn't come in yet. It was nerve-racking. Croswell and I both thought they were going to

95

convict me on the assault and be hung on the involuntary manslaughter. As we waited, one of the deputies came over and said, "When this is all over, how fast do you want to get out of here?" I said, "As fast as humanly possible." He said, "Okay. I know exactly where we'll go."

The jury came back in, and the judge said, "No matter what this verdict is, there will be no outburst in this courtroom." I looked around, and there were deputies everywhere. The courtroom was overflowing. Judge Nurre then looked at the charge sheet and handed it back to the bailiff, who gave it to one of the clerks.

They read the verdict for the first count, assault. "Not guilty."

On the charge of involuntary manslaughter, they were hung.

I looked at Croswell and said, "What did they say?" He didn't hear me.

He looked over at me and said, "This is the damnedest thing I've ever seen in my life."

I said, "What did they say?"

He said, "Not guilty."

I said, "Did they say "guilty?" That's what we expected them to say. I had my mind ready for the worst. If twelve people said I did it, then fine, I would stand in front of the man and take what was coming to me.

Croswell just had this big smile. I looked back at my wife, and she was crying. I was getting all these mixed signals, and I said, "What the heck just went on?"

Then the judge asked the jury foreman, "Would further deliberation help you with the charges?"

And he replied, "No. I don't think so."

Judge Nurre then declared a mistrial because jurors could not agree on whether I was guilty of involuntary manslaughter. I was disappointed he did not dismiss the charge outright based on what he heard in the trial. Anyway, I was a free man.

And we were finished. The case was over. As I stood up, a deputy walked over and grabbed me by the hand and said, "Let's go." And out the door we went. My family followed, and we went down the back stairwell. I don't remember hitting one step. I reached the basement and there was Brian with my truck.

I got in the driver's seat, Brian and Kristen's mom jumped in the back seat, Kristen jumped in the front seat. I hit the gas, and we drove down to Aberdeen, where there is a restaurant called Brown's, which I knew would be far enough away. No one would know where I was. That's where we had our victory dinner, for lack of a better term. I don't remember getting there, I don't remember eating, and I don't remember going home. I couldn't tell you how fast we were going. I know that's where we went, I know that's where we ate. I know we went home afterwards. The whole thing was surreal.

Chapter 12

Pavlov's Dogs

Animals with a conditioned response. A long time ago, there was a scientist by the name of Pavlov. For one of his experiments, he would ring a bell before he fed his dogs. After several weeks, Pavlov would ring the bell and then not feed his dogs right away. The dogs started salivating even though there was no food. Given a specific set of conditions, Pavlov reasoned, the animal would respond a certain way.

The leaders and press in Cincinnati are conditioned as well. Of course, there was strong reaction to my verdict. Here's a sampling: Rev. J. W. Jones of the Greater New Mount Moriah Missionary Church in Carthage said, "I'd hoped the city would be just, that somewhere along the line people would have the inclination to do the right thing." Avondale resident Nashid Shakir said, "Black life means nothing. All we want is equity. We want a piece of this town. We want inclusion. All we get is our children arrested. Somewhere there is going to be justice."

It's easier to blast a white cop than to admit the obvious: that black-on-black crime is out of control in Cincinnati. Mayor Luken, ever the politician, said, "The key to this is getting more proactive policing with community involvement." The key to what?

He and the city received exactly what they asked for by the way they handled themselves and their community. City Manager John Shirey remarked, "I am surprised by the outcome." Shirey hadn't given me a fair hearing when I was suspended without pay. I knew he hadn't really looked at the evidence.

Prosecutor Mike Allen said, "We're satisfied with the job that the jury did. They asked a lot of questions of the judge, and in no way shape or form are we critical of the jury." He added, "Convicting a police officer in Hamilton County is difficult. It's an uphill battle."

City Council member Phil Heimlich was one of the few supportive public officials. He said, "I think we have a system and we have to respect that system. The jury came back with (a verdict) and we have to respect that."

My attorney said of me, "He's thrilled that he's been vindicated in the portion that's been decided." "I think it's very unfair." He continued, "I think the Cincinnati Police Department gets a bum rap. It's easy to second-guess an officer involved in a physical (confrontation)."

Later, Croswell said the acquittal on the assault charge and the 10-2 vote on the manslaughter charge showed that the evidence against me was not convincing. Thankfully, the demonstrators that had been outside the courthouse and all through the city did not make their threatened response. There was no more rioting. The city stayed calm.

Of course, all the activists and the deceased's family wanted to know if Allen was going to ask for a re-trial. Allen would only say that if there was a re-trial, he would present the same case against me. He added, "The key difference would be the jury. Different juries are different. You never know what a jury is going to do." In other words, there was nothing wrong with the prosecution's case; the jurors were to blame for me walking free. But then, he admitted that the witnesses had been "inconsistent."

When asked if I would be re-tried, Allen did the politically correct thing, saying he would meet with his top assistants, Piepmeier and Longano, to decide if there would be a second trial for involuntary manslaughter. He added, "I want to do it quickly. The Owensby family needs closure, as does the Jorg family. I don't want to keep these families waiting any longer."

That same day, October 31, the Post reported that two jurors thought I was guilty of involuntary manslaughter. The paper also revealed that, the jury voted at least three times and the final count was 10-2 to acquit. Of course, the Post got it wrong when they reported the holdouts were a black man and a white man who voted against acquittal. The two jurors were both black --the same two jurors who did not stand up (with the other 10 jurors) to watch Officer Hunter's demonstration with the mannequin, where he showed how I had my hand around Owensby's forehead. The female juror who voted against acquittal said she could not go home and tell her family and friends she voted "not guilty". She was afraid.

I will never understand how two jurors voted "not guilty" on the assault charge, yet voted "guilty" on involuntary manslaughter. After all, they needed the assault conviction to get a conviction on involuntary manslaughter.

From the prosecutor down, they swore to find the truth and render a fair verdict, but it was a facade. And I lived in fear while they played politics. How far would it all go?

On November 1, the Owensbys and their attorneys publicly stated that federal officials should take over the prosecution of the officers involved in their son's arrest. The Post reported their concerns over, "possible obstruction of justice" by Cincinnati police. The Owensbys told reporters, "From the start we only wanted justice for our son. We wanted to trust the system and let it work. The riots didn't have to start in April. They could have started in November, but we said no. We would let the system work, and it has failed us."

The Owensby's wanted Pat and I charged with criminal offenses in federal court so local prosecutors would not have jurisdiction. They contended that Allen told them in a private meeting during the trial that he would retry the case if there was a mistrial.

On November 7, the Owensby family filed a Federal lawsuit, in which they claimed that their son was, "assaulted, tortured and killed." The suit sought damages in excess of $75,000 and demanded a jury trial. Dozens of defendants were named, including the police chief, myself, and Pat.

The Owensby family must have filed the suit after reading the Post, which had reporters in the courtroom every day of my trial, who continued to report bad information.

One article stated: "Owensby was being questioned by police inside the store when he bolted, was tackled by officers and died in the ensuing struggle."

For the seventh time, we never spoke to Owensby in the store, only one officer tackled Owensby, and he did not die in the struggle!

The Owensbys were clearly angry about the way Allen's office had prosecuted me.

They were furious when Allen announced that there wouldn't be a second trial. On November 8, the day after the reelection of Mayor Charlie Luken and two City Council members who had called for my head, Alicia Reece and Paul Booth, I learned that I would not be retried. Allen said discussions with investigators, witnesses and one of the jurors from my trial all indicated that another trial would be pointless. In announcing the decision, Allen said it was, "Because we have little chance of winning a conviction".

While this was not what Mr. Owensby wanted to hear, the press adopted a sympathetic tone in discussing Allen's decision not to retry me. The press concluded that the prosecutor faced a difficult task the first time he tried to convict me, and that a guilty verdict would be even harder to come by in a second trial. The primary reason: because I was found "not guilty" on the assault charge. That verdict blew the prosecution's entire case out of the water, since they had alleged that Roger Owensby died because I assaulted him.

The Enquirer, which continued to erroneously report that "Several officers tackled Mr. Owensby," ran an editorial with the headline, "Retrial could be futile." They reviewed the jury's findings, Allen's dilemma, the protests of those who alleged unfair treatment of blacks, and concluded, "The verdict on Officer Jorg is not satisfying to anyone, but it's not likely a second trial will achieve anything."

The Post took a stronger stance in an editorial headlined, "The Death of Roger Owensby." Post editorial writers railed, "we nonetheless find the outcome incredible--and some of the actions described at the trial revolting. We do believe that Hamilton County Prosecutor Mike Allen should retry Jorg on the involuntary manslaughter charge. It deserves to be settled. We also believe the Justice Department should review the Owensby death to determine if federal prosecution is warranted."

Allen must have felt pressure, because he released a statement defending his office: "I know personally that my office, including my most senior prosecutors and victim/witness staff, has worked with the Owensbys every step of the way in this laborious and painful criminal process. I also know that the prosecutors who handled the case, both seasoned veterans of literally hundreds of homicide trials, gave this case their very best. We seek to continue to reach out for input from the Owensbys in the important decision of whether to retry Officer Jorg."

Police Chief Streicher also covered his tracks. He insisted that his detectives fully investigated Owensby's death and turned all their findings over to the prosecutor's office. Streicher then said he didn't have a problem with the Owensbys' wanting the federal government to investigate.

I should have been on the top of the world. I was working again. Even though it was at the impound unit, I had my badge and gun, and I was allowed to be myself again.

Unfortunately, the feeling of being free only lasted about two days. I was working a special security detail the day Vice President Cheney came to Cincinnati. I was approached by a lieutenant from Cincinnati Police Intelligence Section. I was informed that the intelligence unit had reliable information that Mr. Owensby, Sr. had made death threats against me.

I wasn't worried at first, but then the lieutenant told me that they were informed by Mr. Owensby's psychiatrist that Owensby stated, "I have a gun and I will get justice." The intelligence section lieutenant told me that they were staking out where I was working and that they had photos of Mr. Owensby waiting there while I was working.

Now I was beginning to be frightened. Every day I went to work, I had to look over my shoulder. The impound lot is in a dark, secluded area of town. I was often scheduled to close the lot alone. I began taking different routes home to see if someone was following me, I was paranoid.

The arrival of a subpoena compelling me to give my deposition to Owensby family lawyers made me realize that my ordeal was far from over. Their suit meant I would have to defend myself all over again.

I was a jumble of emotions on the day I had to give my deposition to four or five of the attorneys for their civil case. Roger Owensby, Sr., and his wife, were also present. Pat came down with me for protection. He was a great help to me that day. I don't know how I would have survived all these years if it hadn't been for him!

From the beginning, I fought to keep my frustration and anger in control. At first, I just told my story, giving matter-of-fact "yes" and "no" answers when questioned. I didn't want to be there, and I was cooperating, but I wanted them to have to work hard to get what I had to say. I wasn't giving the attorneys any more than they asked. Then they dug into the right questions. I went on emotionally for about 35 minutes. At the end of it, I was bawling. I left the conference room. I dropped my microphone on the table and walked out of the office. I couldn't stand being talked to in such a manor that made police officers look like we were some kind of brute squad.

I resented being face-to-face with Mr. Owensby. I tried to pretend he wasn't there, but it didn't work.

After leaving the interview, I stood in the hallway and called Dr. Daum, the police psychologist. I tried to talk to him about what I was experiencing. I wanted to leave the deposition. I didn't want to have to explain myself to them. But he made me realize that I didn't have a choice. I went back into the interview with a new perception. I was going to help the Owensby family out in their law suit against the city. I was going to tell them every way I knew of that the city played games with them as well as me.

I was upset, because I had to talk about things I didn't want to talk about. I had to tell them how I did everything by the book and how their son had made it into so much more than it needed to me. That's the killer, that I didn't do anything wrong. I should have been glowing as I talked, but I wasn't. I fought with myself saying, "Why am I condemning myself for something I had no control over?"

I lost control again later in the deposition. The Owensby's attacked me personally, privately; they attacked everything I've ever done. That is when I told them that the city was playing both sides. I told them that they were doing the right thing, and that I hoped they got paid in their lawsuit. I also told them that they can sue the city all they want for what has happened, but that they should drop the officers from the suit. I don't think they were expecting me to say that.

When it was all said and done, and the attorneys turned the microphones off and stopped the video camera, they stood up, and Mr. Owensby walked out. He made a comment under his breath I couldn't make out as he left.

Mrs. Owensby stayed in the room. As I was standing up, she approached me and looked at me. Her attorney was next to her, and my attorney was behind me.

I said, "Ma'am, I may be overstepping my bounds. My attorney is probably going to kill me..." And I looked over at her attorney, over my shoulder to my civil attorney, Don Hardin. He backed up, probably knowing then he wasn't going to be able stop me.

I turned to Mrs. Owensby, and said, "I think you need to hear this. I can't bring your son back. I don't know why he died that night. He shouldn't have

103

died that night, and he does not deserve a death sentence. But none of the officers here did anything to cause it. And, I think once we fully get into this, you will realize that, too."

I told her, "I'm sorry it took me so long to be able to tell you all these things, and to basically apologize for what happened to your son. But I want you to know that none of the officers intentionally, maliciously or with criminal minds did anything to harm your son. And I'm sorry it took this long for you to hear that from somebody. But I am not responsible for the death of your son, and neither are any of the officers."

When I finished, she asked me, "Why did it take you three years to tell me this?"

I said, "I may be overstepping my bounds again." I looked at my attorney and said, "Ma'am, from day one, I was told never to say anything. Those were not my wishes, but my attorneys', my criminal attorney, and now my civil attorney. This is the first chance I had in three years to say anything."

Then her husband made a nasty comment to me and she cut him off, saying, "Go wait in the hall. He's making sense."

I shook her hand and said, "I hope we can get this over quickly." And she walked out.

The whole deposition was unnerving, especially coming face-to-face with Roger Owensby, Sr. He was adamant that his son didn't "bolt and run", even though the video from the store showed that's exactly what happened. He insisted, "Jorg had to say something to him for him to run." It was Officer Hunter saying, "Cuff him" that sent Roger Owensby running that night.

So, I hadn't been keen on talking to Mr. Owensby. I was on edge. And the feeling was clearly mutual. The tension between us was obvious. But I could talk to his wife and I think I made some headway. I understand they are still angry. I'm angry, too. I told them in my deposition that they were being used. The prosecutor promised them certain things that he never delivered. The prosecution and other officials promised they would do certain things to me, or that they would ask me certain things. They said they'd do this and that, and they didn't follow through.

After giving my deposition, I told Pat, who had gone with me to support me and keep me under control, "I don't know how I'm going to do this (tell my story) again."

And he said, "If you do, tell it that way at trial; there is no way someone is ever going to question you about this again."

I said, "Pat, I don't want to go to trial. I don't ever want to do this again."

It's hard to describe how I felt. A jury had acquitted me, yet I had to defend myself all over again. It was maddening. I didn't do anything wrong, and if I could make people understand that, I'd be on the road to recovery. But I couldn't. It's been five years, and I still can't figure it out how to prove that I didn't kill a man.

Maybe I analyze things too much. I analyze what happened everyday and I keep coming up with the same conclusion. But that's not good enough for me. Maybe I'd have a measure of peace if I could find something wrong with what I did. Because at least then, being accused and tried would have some reason behind it.

Pat and I had both been cleared of wrongdoing by a jury, but we continued to be hot property. Not only had the Owensbys filed a civil suit against me, but the Black United Front was demanding a re-trial and insisting that Allen appoint a special prosecutor from a list of candidates supplied by black leaders.

Chapter 13

Honest Cops

There was a lot of pressure on the police officers who responded to the incident outside Sam's Sunoco on November 7, 2000. The five who had direct contact with Roger Owensby--myself, Pat, Officer Hunter, Officer Hodge, and Officer Sellers--underwent hours of questioning by the internal investigation section.

My interview at Internal lasted three hours. I was asked if I saw Owensby put anything in his mouth. "No." I was asked if he spit up anything during the struggle. "No." But I wasn't anywhere near Owensby during the final minutes of his life. I didn't place him in the car. I didn't see him again until after he had been taken out of the car and efforts were underway to save his life. But it's interesting that Internal asked me if I saw him put anything in his mouth. It was clear that they knew Owensby spit up when EMTs were trying to revive him.

I was also asked if I reported "use of force" to my commanding officer. I said that we had requested a boss because of the macing, and that I had mentioned the head wrap to Sergeant Watts. I explained that we had intended to tell Sergeant Watts exactly what happened at the scene, but before we could do so, the sergeant asked, "Where is he?" So we walked over to the Golf Manor car, opened the door to talk to Owensby and then we did what we had to do. We turned our attention to something that was a heck of a lot more important than saying, "Hey Sarge, let me tell you about..."

The way it all broke down, yes, there was time to report use of force, but it wasn't a necessity at the time. Was it going to be reported? Yes. But unfortunately it did not get done. Priorities dramatically changed when we saw Owensby was unconscious.

I can almost hear my critics saying, "Yeah, sure you were going to report use of force. To them I say, "I've always been honest." It's like I told my attorneys; "If you want to find some dirt on me, I'll be the first one to tell you when I mess up." I found out a long time ago that if you lie about something or shortchange somebody or don't tell the whole truth, it's going to come back and bite you worse than if you just reported what happened in the first place. Integrity means everything to me. If I screw up, I'm going to come forward. I'd rather go that way than wait for someone to find out.

Here's an actual example: One day I was running radar. I stopped a woman, and was writing a ticket when an officer about three blocks away called for assistance. I ran up to the woman's car and told her, "I'll drop the ticket off at your house" and was off. I went to the assistance run and totally forgot about going to her house. About two days later, my boss, Sergeant Gillespie asked me, "Did you stop a lady…?"

"Well, I stopped a lot of cars that day, Sarge." I told her, "You have to be a little more specific."

So she described it. Then I knew, so I responded, "Yeah, I stopped her."

"Where's the ticket?" she asked.

"Oh no. I bet it's still in my ticket book." So I went out to my car, and sure enough, there's her ticket and her drivers license. I walked inside, set the ticket book on the counter and said "I totally forgot." and explained what happened. She told me to take it over to the woman's house. So I did, apologized to the woman for my mix-up and came back to the office.

When I got back to the district I went to Sergeant Gillespie expecting to have to sign off on a disciplinary entry in my personnel file.

"Where's my ESL?"

She said, "Don't worry about it. But you can't forget to do that stuff."

I've always done everything by the book. I'm not a saint, just one of many honest cops who strive to hold themselves to a high standard. Most cops are honest and conscientious. Police officers are trustworthy. But they also have a strong self-preservation instinct. That was obvious in my case. When things got hot, when it became clear that Pat and I were going down, everybody covered themselves. Nobody wanted to go down with us.

After Owensby had been placed in the Golf Manor car that night, officers began congratulating each other on a good arrest. One officer was giving high fives: "This is cool. This is awesome."

That's what I saw. I wasn't celebrating. I was telling Sergeant Watts what happened. But some of the other guys were excited about how "we" took this guy down.

Five minutes after Owensby was pulled out of the car however, nobody had anything to do with it. They were saying, "Pat and Blaine did this." That's the stance some of them maintained even when they were being questioned by Internal: "Nope, I wasn't there when Caton and Jorg were fighting him." And, "Someone else walked him to the car. It wasn't me."

For example, Officer Sellers also denied walking Owensby to the car, but Golf Manor Officer Heiland told detectives that Sellers had blood on his shirt. That's the only time he could have gotten blood on his shirt. He didn't assist in the handcuffing. More than one officer saw Sellers walk Owensby to the car. Officer Brian Menefee told them, "a black officer" helped Jorg. That had to be Sellers or Hunter.

Somebody's lying. And I don't think it's Heiland and Menefee. What do they have to gain by lying about Sellers and Hunter? Absolutely nothing. A lot of lies were thrown around when Owensby died.

This really irks me: at Internal, when every officer was trying to distance himself from the situation, Sellers said, "Well, I knew Owensby was in a bad situation. I knew he was hurt."

So the enduring question I have for him is, "Why didn't you do anything about it?"

An interesting thing about Sellers is that he was so concerned with covering himself, yet he never said a bad word about me. Sellers notices race. If a white guy does something wrong, he'll be the first one to report it. But, he said he saw everything I did, and that I did nothing wrong. And he said Pat hit Owensby two more times than he (Sellers) would have, but that wasn't necessarily wrong. So in this particular situation, Sellers never cried "racism." Nor did he call a foul, saying anything was wrong with what we did.

Only a handful of people did the right thing and told the truth: Myself and Pat, Officers Lawson, Hodge, and Spellen. I would say those are all for the cops who were there. A few of the sergeants, Watts and Browner also told the truth. Sergeant Browner was accused of calling Lieutenant Luebbe that night and telling him Owensby died of a chokehold. But Sergeant Browner maintained, "I never made that phone call. You can check my phone log."

She did call Lieutenant Luebbe to request the Criminal Investigation Section and Homicide units. But she never mentioned a chokehold.

Transcripts of interviews of Officers Hodge, Spellen, Hasse and Lawson are very revealing. They stand out in the stark contrast to the, "I'm not sure... I heard someone say, but I didn't see it. I didn't walk the prisoner" statements made by officers and civilians alike. Here are the words of four honest men:

Jason Hodge

Officer Hodge is an undercover officer who was at the scene. He's also in the army and served in Iraq. Hodge's interview with homicide detectives almost matches mine word-for-word. In a previous chapter, I recounted how detectives tried to bully Officer Hodge into going along with what the coroner and media claimed happened. But Hodge wouldn't waver. He boldly told the truth and was adamant about what he did and didn't see. Investigators threatened to charge Hodge with conduct unbecoming of an officer and lying under oath. They slammed him in his Internal interview, wanting him to implicate me and Pat. He suffered for weeks before they finally let him go. Here are some excerpts from what I would call his interrogation, his interview:

Q: "At any time did you see anybody on his (Owensby's), on his back -- I mean physically sitting on his back or laying on his back, putting pressure on him to keep from fighting?"

Hodge: "No, I just, like I said, I just saw Caton and Jorg trying to push his arms towards the middle. That's all."

Q: "Do you remember them having their knee in his back, or do you remember anybody hitting him with a fist?"

Hodge: "No."

Q: "At any time did you see anybody on his head, trying to hold his head down?"

Hodge: "No."

Q: "Did you see anybody around his throat?"

Hodge: "No."

Q: "Did you see anybody with an arm around his neck?"

Hodge: "No."

Q: "Or his head?"

Hodge: "No."

Q: "Did you see anybody trying to push his head down to keep his head still?"

Hodge: "No."

Q: "You're telling us nobody being on top of him. They're all being, they're on the side of him. Everybody is on the side of him."

Hodge: "Mm-hmm, that's what I saw when I got there. I mean, I'm not, I'm here to tell you right now, I'm not gonna lie for anybody. I'm not going to prison for anybody. I'm not losing my job for anybody. My family is the number-one importance here and that's one of the reasons why I'm making this statement, to clear my name."

Q: "You don't remember seeing anybody with an arm or PR 24 or anything around this guy's head or neck area?"

Hodge: "When I came up, no."

Q: "You don't remember seeing anybody with anything on top of the guy's head, holding his head down on the ground?"

Hodge: "No."

Q: "And you don't remember seeing anybody actually on top of Owensby's body?"

Hodge: "No."

Finally, Hodge became fed up.

"I don't know what more to say," he said. "I mean there's, I don't know what else, really. I mean, I told you everything I saw."

Officer Alex Hasse

Hasse's notes from November 7, 2000 read: "Arrived after subject in custody in rear of Golf Manor unit. Assisted in pulling him out of car. Performed a head tilt, began chest compressions, CPR. Once Fire was on scene and took over, I noticed a crack like substance on the subs chin and cheek. Myself and P.O. Hodge secured the substance and placed it in a property envelope. "

During the interview, Hasse said: "Next thing I know is officer (on the radio) needs assistance. My partner ran over, I stayed with the prisoner. I got to where I could at least see what they were doing. They were behind a car, but some Huntington Meadows security officers (were) on the scene, looking at them. Sellers ran over after the assistance was out. I walked over. Sergeant Watts was there, (Owensby) was not responding. Officer Caton and I took him out of the vehicle. I commenced chest compression. We did CPR until the Fire Department came, have no idea how long he was in the back of the car. Assistance was canceled prior to my going over there.

Hasse: "As they (fire) were suctioning, I noticed a white substance on his (Owensby's) chin. We got the property envelope, we got off what we could off of his chin and neck and put it in the property envelope."

Q: "When the struggle was taking place, do you recall seeing any civilian witnesses standing in the area?"

Hasse: "No."

Q: "How was he (Owensby) positioned in the car?"

Hasse: "On his stomach. I believe his face was towards the rear seat. His head was on the driver's side."

Q: There's been no discussion on that relief, can you elaborate on that kind of conversation?"

Hasse: "Just kind of casual conversation that goes on after this type of incident, based on what the news had published, since that's about all we knew. You know the paper said it was a chokehold. Whether it was a chokehold or choke, or whether he fell on his fist, since he was trying to put crack in his mouth, you know what, we we're all just kind of throwing ideas around."

Q: "During the point of your CPR, you made reference to a white substance like vomit is coming out of his mouth."

Hasse: "Actually, during the CPR, when I had the mask on him, every time I would blow a breath in I would hear a gurgling as the air expired back out. So I could tell that the airway was block(ed) with either blood or some other substance, I did not know this until Fire Department was there, using the suctioning device to clear out his airway. As they were doing that is when I saw what I thought, or think, is crack that came out of his airway."

Q: "Anybody admit striking the individual, punching him?"

Hasse: "No."

Q: "We've got witnesses, basically civilian witnesses... being punched in the ribs, basically jab him with PR 24 in the ribs. Struck across the back of legs and stuff. And again, hey, that's all within policy and procedure to get somebody to submit to being handcuffed and resisting arrest. And nobody made any reference to any incidents like that to you?"

Hasse: "No. They only mentioned the PR 24 is what I said. I believe it was Officer Hodge stating that he used it to pry out his (Owensby's) arm."

Q: "Anybody, any of them make any reference to choking the guy out, or anything like that?"

Hasse: "No. I never heard anything about that."

Q: "What did Menefee basically say to you?"

Hasse: "The guy was on the ground. He didn't state any specifics as to who was in what position. I believe I asked him if anyone had used a choke hold or anything like that. As I recall, he said, 'No.' He just remembers seeing Officer Caton struck the individual in the back (of the ribs)."

Officer Abe Lawson, plainclothes

Lawson: "He was face down and they were attempting to place handcuffs on him."

Q: "Did you notice a struggle between the suspect an these officers?"

Lawson: "Absolutely. He was resisting."

Q: "Did you hear anything?"

Lawson: "All I heard was, "Stop resisting, put your hands behind your back." He was maced. He was pretty much standing up on his own, but he was being guided basically by the officers."

Q: "Were his feet touching the ground?"

Lawson: "Yes. Officer Brazile approached the car, just to check on this guy, told Golf Manor, didn't appear like this guy was breathing."

Q: "He's handcuffed, he's picked up to be transported to the uniform police car, correct?"

Lawson: "Correct."

Q: "And to the best of your knowledge he was, was walking or his feet were touching the ground as he was being taken to the, he wasn't physically picked up?"

Lawson: "No."

Q: "Best you could tell he was being assisted to the police car?"

Lawson: "Correct. His feet were touching the ground."

Q: "Did you remember was he seated when they put him in the car, or was he laying on the back seat?"

Lawson: "He was seated."

Q: "Did you see anybody with a headlock on Mr. Owensby?"

Lawson: "No."

Q: "At any time did you see anybody with a, what they call a chokehold, on Mr. Owensby?"

Lawson: "No."

Q: "Were any of the these officers totally laying on top of Mr. Owensby?"

Lawson: "No."

Victor Spellen

Officer Spellen has been honest all the way through these events, even though he was accused of lying. He didn't. Spellen was fired for allegedly telling one story to the grand jury and a different story in court. But Spellen didn't change his story, he told it two different ways; when he tried to explain this, he was told the interview was over. Spellen wanted to explain the discrepancies, but he wasn't given the opportunity.

The discrepancies appeared when interviewers compared his testimony to the video tape from his cruiser. During the first interview, Spellen had in his mind what happened, never realizing he had the whole thing on tape from his car. He never put the two together. He stuck to his story all the way through. Spellen didn't tell a different story in court, he allegedly used "softer" language. He was fired for admitting that he lied at Internal, not at the trial. But did he ever actually acquiesce?

Actually, it's only in the transcript from the Internal interview that Spellen "admits" to lying. According to the written transcript, Spellen says, "Maybe I lied... It was intentional." I listened to the audio tape the transcript was made from, and that statement was not there. But it is in the written report. To me, that makes the entire transcript suspect.

Spellen was my recruit. A nice guy, a little naive, not very strong-willed. Could be leaned on very easy. That tendency resulted in him telling investigators that he saw me demonstrate a hold to Sgt. Watts after the struggle. Spellen said my demonstration lasted, "...maybe a short second." I don't know why he said he saw something he didn't. When I described the struggle to handcuff Owensby to Sgt. Watts, I described it verbally.

Maybe Victor just got caught up in the moment during his interview with Internal. Maybe he felt he had to give them something to get them off his back about the portion of the video that shows him high-fiving other officers after the arrest. Or maybe they caught him off guard. When you start firing a bunch of questions at Victor, you can rattle him very easily. He would have admitted to stealing the Lindbergh baby if they asked him.

Chapter 14

Broken Toys

The sense of satisfaction I felt when I was given my badge back lasted until I had a meeting with Chief Streicher. Caton, Steve Roach and myself were to attend. It was at that meeting we learned that we were being reassigned to the Impound unit. Chief Streicher said it was for our own protection. He also told us he was proud of the way we had handled ourselves through, "all of this," and that we were heroes who would be praised in the future. I had no desire to work in the Impound unit, but I didn't have any choice.

Just as I expected, the Impound unit was miserable. We called it, "The Island of Misfit Toys." Pat was the elephant who had blue spots. I was Yukon Cornelius. We had different names for different officers; the choo choo train with square wheels, and the airplane that didn't fly. That's who got sent to Impound, the toys nobody wanted to play with. We were castoffs, basically police without authority. We were told that if something happened at the counter not to handle it, but to call for District Five and let them handle it.

It wasn't long before we had an incident. Steve Roach and I were working down at Impound when a man came in and demanded his car back. When we wouldn't give it to him, he started knocking things over in our little office. I realized, I can't go out and confront him, because I was told not to. So I can't do anything. Steve and I just looked at each other as the guy tore things up. Then Steve called District Five. By the time they got there, the man was gone. It was almost comical. We had to just sit and watch him tear everything up.

What's worse, Pat and I became the butt of jokes. One night there was a news report that President Bush choked on a pretzel, but was doing fine. The next morning, we showed up at work and someone said, "Did you hear about President Bush?" Another officer said, "were Caton and Jorg there?"

At first I laughed it off, because I knew people were just trying to be funny. But it got old. There is a music group I love to listen to called The Smiths and they have a song titled, "That Joke Isn't Funny Anymore." And these jokes weren't funny. They were too close to home, too near the bone. After a while I wasn't willing to let it pass. I lashed out at a lot of people. Kristen was my first victim unfortunately. Then other officers I worked with, then family members.

Being in the Impound lot was degrading. The work needed to be done, but it should have been done by somebody who wanted to be there. I didn't want to be there. I wanted to be back on the street. I had been vindicated. I didn't see any reason why I shouldn't return to the job I had been doing. I wanted to go back. But my superiors wouldn't let me.

So I improvised. I started working off-duty details enforcing traffic, since I loved to run radar. I ran traffic even though policing now scared the heck out of me. I worked three details before I realized, "I can't be on the street anymore." With the way people were treating me in the station, I no longer felt like I belonged. Former friends treated me differently.

For instance, one day I walked into District Two to see Sergeant Holbrook about working details. Another sergeant was there, and he started choking and gagging and said, "Oh, my God, I'm choking to death," and looked at me and smiled. I thought, "Why are you treating me like this?" He thought it was funny. Tasteless jokes. I heard all kinds.

The officers who were close to me treated me well. They would stop down at the impound lot and talk to me. Their phone calls never seemed to stop. People were calling and congratulating me on my acquittal, telling me they knew I'd be back on top. "Can't wait to have you back in District Four" They would say. I couldn't wait, either. But it never happened.

Pat was fortunate; he left the Impound unit after a couple of weeks. He was assigned to District One. But he didn't forget the other "unwanted toys". I was always happy to see him when he would swing by to talk to me on the way to and from work.

Shortly after Pat left, I became invisible. Fellow officers were telling me they were not to have any more contact with me. Everything stopped, including the visits and the phone calls. I don't know where or how the word came down. I could never find out. One person told me, "We were told we can't talk to you anymore, and if we do, we get in trouble."

I figured it had to come from pretty high up, so I requested a meeting with the Chief of Police. I told Chief Streicher I would never do anything to mar the integrity of the department, or damage its reputation. I reminded him that during my career I had always tried to make things better.

"I don't know why this is coming down on me." I told him.

He patted me on the back and said, "Blaine, it will be fine, everything will be okay."

Apparently, Steve Roach also had a heart-to-heart talk with Chief Streicher. The minute Roach left the department, the chief publicly shot him down and treated him badly in the media. I knew he would do the same thing if I left.

It dawned on me that my situation was never about guilt or innocence. The Owensby incident was merely the straw that broke the political camel's back. The department and city caved in on me because representatives of the black community demanded that something be done. The terrible irony is that I embarrassed the city not because I had been negligent, but because I had followed my training to a "T" and done my job well.

That's why I don't like politics. If the police chief and the city leaders would have done the right thing from the beginning, they wouldn't have the trouble in Cincinnati they have now. I want people to understand that. When I was indicted, it set in motion events that would damage the city for years to come. Now that the truth is coming out, it's looking very bad for those decision makers.

When officers stopped talking to me, it put into concrete that my ordeal wasn't over, and never would be as long as I stayed with this police department. When Internal had started coming around to "investigate" my conduct in the Owensby incident, I said to myself, "I don't want to say anything. I don't want to give them the pleasure of the upper hand. They were at the trial. They know what happened. They probably followed me around for months."

That's when I started looking for another job. From day one, I was told, "Don't say anything," and I figured they didn't need to hear anything now. I was hoping I could get out of this department before I had to say anything to Internal. Now that I realized the game, I wasn't jumping through any more hoops.

Looking back, I think if I would have been allowed to get back into my job, into the work I loved, I would have felt better and healed faster. But depression started to take it's toll. When I was down in the Impound unit, I hated life. I took off more than I actually worked. I burned every bit of sick time, every bit of holiday time. Every chance I had to take off, I took off.

After Pat was sent to District One, my depression intensified. The police department did not want Pat and I sitting in the same place, working the same shift, in the same job space. So they shipped Pat out. I couldn't stand being at Impound wasting time and helping no one wondering when I was going to get out of there. All I ever wanted was to be the best cop I could be. But after the impound lot, it was so difficult to keep a smile on my face and do the job I was supposed to do.

I was out at the firing range one day, talking to a close friend of mine named Jay Weissmann. He's a Christian man. He did a lot of good things for me. He's like my brother. Jay, who is a firearms instructor for another department, was using the Cincinnati firing range. That day, he asked me if I'd consider moving to a different job, "because, you know, things will never be the same again."

He said. I had reached the same conclusion. I said, "If you hear of anything, let me know."

Not many days later, Jay called me at home, and asked me to meet him at the target range. When I arrived, I saw Jay with Denny Dressler, a retired Cincinnati officer I've known since I was a recruit, who was working at the range. Denny took me into the office, shut the door and said, "Jay tells me you are looking for another job."

I told him I was.

He said "I trust that this will go no further." Then he wrote down the name "James Smith, Pierce Township," and the phone number and said, "Call him."

I said, "I don't want to call him cold."

And he said, "How about I call him for you?"

Without hesitation, I said "Call him."

Back at work with Cincinnati, I hated it. I took off so much time just because I hated it. I hated everything about it. In a real twist of reality, I finally had my badge and gun back. I could even work a detail if I wanted to. But by then I hated being a cop. Everything was miserable.

Then Chief Smith called and left a message on my answering machine. He left a great impression on me immediately. When I returned his call he told me to fill out a resume and drop it off to his office. So Brian and I went to Pierce Township. The chief was there, and we started talking. I found a lot to like about him and how he felt about policing. He is a retired Cincinnati Assistant Chief, and a man of very high integrity.

I gave him my resume, and he asked if I wanted to go on a ride-along. I said, "Sure." At this point, my opinion of law enforcement had sunk pretty low. But I went out, and I was absolutely dumbfounded at what I found in Pierce Township. There were two officers on that shift working to cover twenty three square miles! There were only fifteen officers in the entire department including the chief. In Cincinnati, there were two officers to a car in some places and five different districts in the city limits. There, 1300 officers were really not enough to cover the need.

The community was very different from where I had been working in the city. The people there loved the cops. I said, "I've never seen this side of law enforcement before, where people actually wave with all five fingers." It blew me away.

I came back and reported to Chief Smith how much I liked it. There was a new hope for policing inside me. I was determined that I would work in Pierce Township after that day.

Back with the other broken toys at the Impound lot I talked to Pat about whether he was going to stay with Cincinnati.

He said, "Yes, I'm going to stay here."

He was the first person I told that I intended on leaving.

He asked where I could possibly go, because he figured no one was going to hire either one of us.

I told him, "I'm going to Pierce Township."

And he said, "Where in the world is Pierce Township?"

I said, "I just found it the other day."

Shortly after that, there was a message at my house that Chief Smith wanted me to take a polygraph. Thank God! So I went through the interview process and background check. And then Chief Smith told me, "The twelfth of March you will be officially hired. Don't tell anybody that we are going to hire you."

That was fine with me. What Cincinnati didn't know, wouldn't hurt them.

A day or so before I was officially hired at Pierce Township, Internal called me. I had been cleared criminally by the court. Now it was the police department's turn to try my case against their policies and procedures. I called my attorney and told him I didn't want to go. He told me to call in sick.

"But I'm not sick," I said.

He said, "Well, don't show up at work."

I replied, "Then they will fire me." I wanted to leave on my own terms. If I was fired, the Chief could say anything he wanted about why. "So I guess I'm going for the interview with Internal." I told him.

I brought the police FOP attorney with me, and the interview seemed to take forever. It took about three hours. The investigators verbally beat me up, accusing me of all kinds of things. They tried to make me incriminate Pat: "Tell us what Pat really did."

It made me sick. I know they did the same thing with Pat. They did it to everybody involved. "Tell us what Victor did." "Why did he lie for you and Pat?" Why-this-and-why-that. The only reason I endured was the knowledge that I would be leaving in a day.

The next day, I was officially hired at Pierce Township, and I knew I was finally where I wanted to be.

I called Chief Smith and said, "The department is still harassing me."

And the chief said, "You are officially hired, so you can resign."

My first work day at Pierce wouldn't be until April first so I was still working at Cincinnati. When I started my shift that day, I was informed that the Office of Municipal Investigations wanted to talk to me. I called and said, "This is Officer Jorg from the Impound Unit and I understand you want to talk to me today."

"When is a good time?" they asked.

I replied, "There is none. I'm not coming."

They said, "You have to come, you are an employee of the City of Cincinnati."

"No," I replied, "I quit." It felt great.

I went back into the office to report the news to my lieutenant and my sergeant.

"Gentlemen, it's been fun, I quit." I said.

They asked where I was going, and I said, "Read the paper and find out."

At home, I packed up everything that belonged to the City of Cincinnati and threw it in garbage bags. When I went down to Supply to turn in my gear, their eyes were wide. There was still another round of inquisitions and accusations. It was just assumed that I would be there to live through it.

Next, I went to the chief's office, which is right next to Personnel. I was waiting for the sergeant so I could officially sign resignation paperwork, when an assistant chief walked in and said, "Hi, Blaine, how are you?"

I said, "I'm doing fine."

"What are you doing in Personnel?" He said.

I said, "I'm resigning."

"Okay, very good."

He walked away, turned around, and came running back. "You're quitting?!"

I said, "Yup."

And he said, "You can't do that."

And I said, "Yes, I can."

He took off, trying to find the chief. But the chief was in a meeting he couldn't leave. By now, other people were wondering what was going on. Lieutenant Luebbe walked in and said, "You're leaving?"

I said, "Yes."

And he responded, "That's the best thing you could do." Another of the ranking officers looked over his shoulder, gave me the thumbs-up, and said, "Good job."

It was amazing. I left on my own terms, not theirs. I didn't stick around to cooperate with the "investigation", which produced a 79-page report that charged me and seven other officers with violations of department policies, rules, and regulations.

Officers Caton, Hunter, Hodge, Sellers, Spellen, Brazile and Lawson were charged with improper use of force, failure of good behavior, and neglect of duty. Caton was also charged with improper securing, handling, and transportation of prisoners. Spellen was charged with dishonesty. I was charged with improper use of force, failure of good behavior, neglect of duty, and improper securing, handling and transportation of prisoners. I'll address the charges against me one by one:

Improper use of force

The Office of Municipal Investigations noted that, "When officers have a right to make an arrest, they may use whatever force is reasonably necessary to apprehend the offender or effect the arrest and no more. When a chemical irritant is used, the officer(s) will immediately notify a supervisor."

My actions fall under the acceptable definition for when to use force. And we did immediately notify a supervisor about the macing.

According to OMI, the pressure-point hold I used was a violation of the Manual Rules and Regulations and Disciplinary Process, Section One, 1.01

(A) which states: "Members shall not negligently fail to carry out any rule, regulation, procedure, directive, or order of the division, which may lead to risk of physical injury to another or financial loss to the division." This implies that I shouldn't have used the pressure-point technique.

Regarding the mandibular angle pressure point technique I used, OMI investigators stated, "The officer's hand not applying the pressure point, secures the subject's chin." That's not at all an accurate description. If you put your hand by the chin, you can be bitten. The training tape, and the Cincinnati Academy, both state that in the field you use what works. I respectfully suggest that OMI speak with their academy instructors who teach the mandibular angle pressure point technique. They might also want to talk with Sam Faulkner, the State of Ohio's use of force expert, who teaches officers how to subdue subjects with minimal use of force. Basically, while Owensby was resisting the way he was, by not surrendering his hands, I could have delivered punches or kicks. I chose to reduce my level of force to gain compliance.

OMI said my own words sustained the allegation that I utilized improper procedures in applying the mandibular angle pressure point technique on Owensby. I don't know what words they're referring to. The technique I described is permitted and taught. In court, Officer and academy instructor Todd Brunner said the hold as described is permitted.

The OMI report also concluded that, "A preponderance of the evidence indicates Jorg, Caton, Sellers, Hunter and Hodge did not report use of force to their Supervisor when Sergeant Watts arrived on the scene." However, macing was reported. I also reported, "I had his head wrapped almost the whole time. I had my hand across his forehead trying to hold him down on the ground. I also had one of his arms as a restraint move. As I turned to hold him down, he brought his head up. I had to push it back down. He hit his head on the ground. It wasn't an intentional move."

OMI really took a flight of fantasy in concluding that I tried to hide evidence that I used excessive force. The report stated, "Officer Jorg was sufficiently concerned that he destroyed his uniform by having the sleeve cut at the scene." I had placed the sleeve of my shirt in the trunk of my cruiser for safekeeping. I advised Sergeant Watts and Lieutenant Luebbe that I cut my sleeve off and told them why I did. Blood is a contaminant.

Failure of good behavior

The report portrayed me as an out-of-control cop, who lost control, and took out his anger on a suspect. I'm not sure where that myth came from. When Internal asked me in March if I was upset when we were apprehending Owensby, I replied, "No."

But OMI contended, "Officer Jorg acknowledged that he appeared to be angry immediately after the encounter."

The report also stated, "Officer Jorg acknowledged that he appeared to be angry toward Officer Victor Spellen when Officer Spellen asked him what occurred during the encounter." When Spellen had approached and asked what happened, I had replied, "Move."

I wasn't angry; I had just finished being involved in a strenuous struggle with an extremely strong man and I needed to calm down and let the adrenaline flow slow down. I also reported that to Sergeant Watts.

Neglect of duty

Neglect of duty is a laughable accusation in this case. My involvement in the arrest on November 7 was by the book. The report erroneously maintained that Owensby died in a Roselawn parking lot while one Cincinnati police officer knelt on his back with an arm around his head and neck (and handcuffing him at the same time). In detailing the "knee-in-the-back scenario," the report devoted a lot of space to Aerial St. Clair, even mentioning that she passed a polygraph test on November 15, 2000. According to St. Clair, "One of the police officers got on the back of Mr. Owensby and placed his knee in the middle of Mr. Owensby's back. When Mr. Owensby continued to resist, this same police officer placed his arm around Mr. Owensby's throat and held his arm there for approximately ten seconds." As shown earlier, St. Clair was far from a credible witness. And she's the only one who reported seeing a knee in the back.

Interestingly enough, four years later I requested through the "Freeon of Information Act," St. Clair's polygraph answers, and all the questions she was asked, and the city's solicitor advised me that they no longer had the records.

125

The most damning part of the report was the findings of Dr. Cyril Wecht, the "Expert in Anatomic, Clinical and Forensic Pathology, and Legal Medicine" the city had hired to support their case. Wecht concluded "that the cause of death of Roger Owensby, Jr. was mechanical asphyxia due to compression of his chest by Police Officer Robert Blaine Jorg, who was kneeling on his back."

It's important to note that Dr. Wecht reached his conclusion without portions of the trial testimony that supported my version of events or my statement to Internal. Doctor Wecht only had one side of the story. He asked for everything relevant, but he only received what the city wanted him to see.

For instance, the city did not advise him that six witnesses saw Owensby walk to the car. Did anyone tell Dr. Wecht that crack cocaine recovered was from Owensby at the hospital? Or that his shirt had a "white flaky substance" on it? Did he know that witnesses saw that white flaky substance on his chin? Did the city tell Dr. Wecht the Hamilton County Coroner was misled on the length of the struggle? And that there was no vomit at the struggle scene? With the lack of information he had, I can't fault Dr. Wecht.

Dr. Wecht stated in his report, "In the materials provided, I could find no evidence that Mr. Owensby could have walked to the police cruiser under his own power." The key word here is "provided". The city withheld vital information.

Dr. Wecht examined Owensby's anterior neck and noted no hemorrhage on reflecting the strap muscles. He reported, "In the right lateral view of the upper half of the body, the neck and head do seem dark, suggesting the possibility they are congested." He also stated, "In this case, there is a history given by Officer Jorg that he put his weight on Mr. Owensby's back while he applied a 'mandibular angle pressure point.'" In Dr. Wecht's opinion, the hemorrhages (in both sides of Mr. Owensby's back) were created by the complete weight of my weight directed through my knees.

Improper securing, handling and transportation of prisoners

I did not transport Owensby to the car, so I have no idea how I could be charged with improper securing, handling, and transportation of the prisoner. I was picking up my cuffs and PR 24 while Owensby was being secured, handled and placed in Golf Manor police car for transportation. The report even stated, "(Officer) Hunter came in; grabbed Mr. Owensby. And they started walking to the car." Mr. Ayyad, in his statement, said that I "...just stood there..." while other officers walked Owensby to the car.

Pat is quoted as saying "Mr. Owensby placed his feet on the ground and walked to the Golf Manor car, supported by Officers Sellers and myself." OMI noted that Officer Sellers testified: "Officers Caton and Jorg escorted Mr. Owensby to the police vehicle and he walked directly behind them."

I was also faulted for not attending to Owensby after he was placed in the cruiser. Why I should have been the one to assist him isn't explained. I wasn't one of the officers who looked into the car and didn't act when they saw Owensby lying on his side. As can be seen on the video from Spellen's cruiser, I'm the officer whose contaminated shirt sleeve is being cut off, and I'm applying peroxide to clean my arm while a group of other officers are congratulating one another. Certainly there were other policemen who should have attended to Owensby, including the Golf Manor policemen, in whose car Owensby was placed.

The OMI report isn't worth the paper it's written on. The findings are certainly questionable. OMI was just as negligent as the homicide detectives who fouled up the initial investigation. OMI recommended that I not be restored to the police force, and that I be barred from future employment. It was too late. I had already "barred" them as a future employer and I would never return.

Chapter 15

All Five Fingers

I went to work at Pierce Township, and at first I was very sad to leave Cincinnati. I grew up there. But that city was no longer the fun, fulfilling place it once was. Now I knew what I could expect there was not good. At Pierce Township I was with a bunch of country boys, and I knew my experiences would affect how they viewed me, and how we got along. I experienced so much more than them since I worked in a major city. I worked several homicide scenes, probably twenty while in Cincinnati. There was only one homicide ever in Pierce Township.

I had an interview with the trustees the day I was officially sworn in, and not one of them cared about what happened in Cincinnati. They said, "Blaine, you were the best applicant we had." They told me that even though they hired three officers, I was their first choice. They didn't care about what happened in Cincinnati or about anyone else's opinion on the subject. They were just glad they got a good cop out of it. What a breath of fresh air.

I shouldn't have worried about being accepted by other cops, because apparently Chief Smith told every officer there, "If I hear anybody make an off-the-cuff statement pertaining to Blaine's situation, they will be fired."

It felt so good to finally have a chief that supported me outside the confines of his office.

Nobody did anything out of line. It was, "Welcome aboard." And, "Glad to have you here." And, "If there's anything we can do for you ..." And it wasn't an act. They were genuinely good guys. The guys at Pierce are tops in my book.

Of course, the Owensby incident eventually came up. I remember the circumstances as plain as day. I was sitting with Chief Smith and a couple of other officers. One of them, Phil Hauserman, had been hired at the same time I was. We were taking turns putting in our two cents worth about what's wrong in law enforcement. When it came around to Phil, he said that he hates rumor mills, and that cops are the worst sewing circle around.

Mom and me after returning home from my first day at Pierce

"I hate it when cops talk behind other cops' backs," Phil said.

We all agreed.

Then Phil remarked, "You know what it's like, you say something to somebody, and they say something to somebody else, and the next thing you know, you killed somebody."

He looked at me and his face turned ghostly white. The chief's head went into his hands, and Phil yelled, "Sorry!" and got up and left the room. I laughed so hard because he thought he had crossed the line. He came back and apologized profusely.

I said, "I know you weren't directing it to me, you were just caught up in the emotion of a dramatic situation."

He said, "Blaine, I'm so sorry."

I said, "Forget about it."

After I was there a while, the cops I worked with found out I was all business, but I liked to have fun as well. Once they got comfortable with me, they started pressing me about why I came out to Pierce, and why it was done in secret. This didn't bother me. The Chief was trying to protect me from the city, and the news reporters.

Pierce Township was very quiet. It gave me a chance to really work with the community, have fun and enjoy the better parts of law enforcement. Most of the residents I would run into knew who I was and welcomed me with open arms. I was able to do a lot of things that I never got to do in the city. On Sundays, I was the only officer on duty in the morning. So I would take time in between calls and work with the fire personnel. I would ask them about their equipment, how it worked, how to get it out of the truck. I figured that if I was assisting them on a call, I might need to know how to work some of their tools. The fire personnel assisted me with my interest, and they taught me a lot.

I started to receive cards and letters of support, people welcoming me to Pierce. It was refreshing to see that people actually cared about me. At the same time, having all of the "so glad to have you here" started to take a toll on me. The attention kept drumming into my head all that went on in the city. And it was getting harder to deal with. I know the people of Pierce Township meant to be encouraging to me. However, all it did to me was remind me of the horrible nightmare I was trying so hard to forget.

The officers at Pierce helped me out a lot. The officers there have a bond that is so intense. I know they meant well when they made some of their jokes about the city, and they were only trying to help me, but at the same time, it sometimes would remind me of why I had to leave. That was the down side.

Things were going very well in Pierce for the most part, though. I had to adapt to a new way of policing, but that was fine with me. I enjoyed the laid-back atmosphere. It was refreshing.

One night, I was with my coach, an officer who had been with Pierce his entire twelve year career. He was asking me about some of the things I had seen and done. He couldn't believe how much I had experienced in the city.

And then we got a report of a man with a gun in a bar. "Let's go. Let's rock and roll." I told him. And he said, "We just don't walk into these things."

"Why not?" I said. "I'll take point. Let's go." On our way there we got all the information and backup we would need. So when we arrived I just started into the bar. "C'mon. Just watch my back, that's all you got to do." I told the four officers on scene.

My coach said, "He's nuts. He's absolutely nuts. He's walking in there and the guy has a gun."

And I said, "Yeah, that's what we do. We're cops."

We went into the bar, and sure enough, there he was, sitting at the bar. Both of his hands were visible; one hand flat on the bar, the other hand holding a drink. I had the advantage because his back was to me, and I could see his hands. I took a wide turn around him and tapped him on the shoulder. When he turned up to look at me, he shifted one hand down toward his waistband where most people keep their guns. I scooped him right up off his chair, and put him on the floor. His gun fell out onto the floor. I handcuffed him and stood him up-it's over. My partner just looked at me. So I asked "Can you get the gun?"

131

"Oh. Yeah." he said. He picked it up and unloaded it.

As I walked the suspect out of the bar I looked at the other officers and said, "What was so hard about that?"

"We don't get these all that often." one of them said.

Pierce Township is a bedroom community. The citizens are great. They are neighborly, in most cases. There were a couple of places where people often got drunk, and all they wanted to do was fight. As I was putting one such suspect in handcuffs, he said, "You are that Jorg guy, aren't you?"

And I said, "Yeah, what of it?"

He said, "Are you going to take me into an alley and shoot me somewhere?"

I just smiled and said, "Sir, you got the wrong guy. That was Steve Roach."

I put him in the car, shut the door, and we went to jail.

I responded to another call in a trailer park. When I told that suspect that he was under arrest for domestic violence, he said, "I know you."

I said, "So? Turn around and put your hands behind your back."

"What you going to do, choke me?" He said with a sneer.

I said, "No. I'm going to break your nose."

The look on his face seemed to say, "I don't think he's kidding", which is what I wanted him to think. If he was wondering, "Do I test him or do I turn around and put my hands behind my back?" I wanted him to be compelled to choose the peaceful way out.

I pulled out my asp, or collapsible nightstick, extended it and said, "You got two seconds before I bust you in the head." He turned around and put his hands behind his back. I turned my back to him and chuckled to the other officer on scene.

It worked. I wasn't going to hit him, but I wanted him to think I would. I cuffed him and took him to the cruiser. The other cop looked at me and said, "You just threatened him."

"Yeah, I did. But I got him in cuffs didn't I?"

Sometimes it's what you say that can save a situation from erupting. If he had raised his arms in a quick agitated motion, I would have hit him. But I accomplished what I wanted, and nobody got hurt. It seemed to be a win-win situation.

All told, things were better out at Pierce Township, but even there it wasn't final. It wasn't over. I wasn't at peace. About six months into the job I wanted to leave the best job I could have asked for, but my wife and my buddies Brian and Jay convinced me to stay.

I always felt like I was in the spotlight. My new-found friends aren't comfortable with some of the things I do, there were troublemakers on the street who wanted to fight me, and then, reporters started calling me again. In this wonderful new place I worked, all I could see was the half-empty side of things.

One of the Enquirer reporters wanted to do an article on how I was adapting to Pierce Township. That was the last thing I wanted. I was sitting in the chief's office when he returned the call from the Enquirer reporter. Chief Smith said, "Let me put it to you this way, sir. I'm not going to help you write a bad article about one of my cops. Because no matter what I tell you, you will twist it. Thank you for calling and have a nice day" and hung up. That's how he handled it. Every voicemail he got about me from then on, he would delete as soon as he got them.

The press still called to find out where I was living. Since Chief Smith wasn't giving them any information, they tried to follow me home. It was overwhelming. I just wanted to be left alone. I wanted to be a normal, private citizen again.

I was hanging in there, tottering on the brink of fitting in with the department and throwing in the towel. It depended on which day you talked to me.

The tide shifted dramatically one night on a traffic stop. That's when I became a loner. One of the officers had stopped a car with five men in it. There was a warrant attached to the car, so somebody in the car had to be wanted. The officer who made the stop didn't know what to do. I didn't say anything, because I was there for back up. Another Pierce car arrived and a county deputy. Now there were four officers and five suspects.

The officer who made the stop turned around and asked, "What do I do?"

Rather than telling him what to do, I said, "I'll do it." I instructed the first man to get out of the car, patted him down, handed him off to the next Pierce Township officer and said, "Cuff him and sit him down." So he cuffed him and sat him down. As that officer is working with the first suspect, I did the same thing with the rest of the men in the car, one-by-one. The last two I searched, I cuffed and sat down on my own.

"Now, who has ID and who doesn't?" I asked the suspects. We got their licenses and found the wanted man.

"You're up. Get in that car. The rest of you guys, have a good night." I said.

I handled the whole thing by myself. Which was probably a mistake. All my patience and understanding had eroded away. The only thing I could think about was getting the situation under control before there could be a conflict.

From that point on, I was viewed as a prima donna. A former lieutenant informed me, "You're not allowed to handcuff someone unless they're under arrest. You're going to get us sued. You're going to get us in trouble."

It could have been an ugly scene, but the chief backed me up. He said, "No, you are allowed to do that. By law, you can do that. So what did Blaine do wrong?"

The lieutenant said, "Well, I don't like the way he did it."

"But what part, legally, morally, ethically, did he do wrong?"

Silence.

At that point, I began separating from the group. At meal breaks I ate dinner with some of the officers, others I didn't. Then I stopped eating while I was working altogether.

Instead, I spent my down time with one of the officers from New Richmond, which bordered our jurisdiction. Until then, if something went on in Pierce, I was the first person everybody called. But after that point, I was left to myself most of the time. I replaced my time with my co-workers by working with the sheriff's deputies, Amelia officers, Union Township cops. I needed to work with someone who wouldn't talk about Cincinnati.

Later, I told Chief Smith, "The one thing this department is missing is a canine unit."

He said, "There's only fourteen guys, Blaine."

"But it needs a canine unit." I insisted.

He replied, "Well, how many drugs do we find in this township, Blaine?"

I said, "Not many, because you don't have a canine unit, and your guys don't know how to do a traffic stop."

The Chief didn't seem to like that. He said, "What do you mean?"

I said, "How many traffic stops have I made where I found some type of alcohol or narcotic?"

He said, "About every other one you do."

I said, "Okay. How many drugs are the other officers finding on a traffic stop?"

He said, "Very, very few."

I said, "It's not because it's not there, it's because they don't know how to do a traffic stop and ask the right questions."

I just kept hounding him, and hounding him, and hounding him. I found a place that would donate a dog for free, a place that would train it for free, a company that would give us a car to re-do, and dog food for free -- for the life of the dog. There would be no cost to the township whatsoever.

I think Chief Smith appreciated my approach to law enforcement. Maybe he also knew that I was struggling to handle the attention that came out of the Owensby incident. He made me the training officer. I got to advise officers what classes they needed and what techniques could be used. I was able to re-focus on something besides that night, but still being a police officer wasn't fun anymore.

I became unmotivated. I started feeling nervous on the job. That's when I knew it was time to quit. I didn't know what the problem was, but I knew I had to get out. I went to see the chief. He tried to talk me out of leaving, and it worked for a while.

Then the Black United Front announced that they were going to have a protest march in Pierce Township on the two-year anniversary of Roger Owensby's death. The Black United Front, the black Baptist ministers, Reverend Damon Lynch, and a group of other activists, were coming to Pierce Township to put me back into the spotlight.

Fortunately for me, Chief Smith is an absolute genius. I was scheduled to work on November 7, but I wanted to take the day off. The chief denied my time off. He told me, "You're not going to be off, you're going to work. But you are not going to be around here. You can go anywhere in this town, but don't be here."

When they came to protest, the chief had plain clothes observers, and had officers from other departments helping out. He locked every door in the municipal building, and told everyone at work that day, "This is private property. If someone doesn't have an appointment, you are not to let them in. Lock the door. Period. Lock the door."

The protestors chanted, "The doors were open for Jorg, the doors were open for Jorg." But nobody was out there to listen to them. All the other officers were inside in case they broke the doors down.

Chief Smith said, "If they break in, they will go to jail. Period. But we are not going to give them any reason to come back."

Somehow, one of the firehouse doors was open. The fire department leads to the police department, which opens to the main building. There was a breach of security and the protestors got inside. Chief Smith met them halfway into the police department. They were chanting, raving, and yelling, but Chief Smith got them to settle down.

Reverand Lynch had a copy of the OMI report that had leveled the procedural charges against me. He kept waving it at Chief Smith. "Read this, read this, read this."

And Chief Smith said, "I don't have to read it. I've already got a copy."

"Well, fine, what did it say?" Lynch was trying to put him on the spot.

What a memory. Chief Smith said, "Turn to page 73, article 17, and you will see in there that Officer Jorg did nothing wrong." The protesting died out at that point. They escorted Lynch out, and that was the end of it.

How Chief Smith shut the protest down was phenomenal. Of course, at the time, I wasn't aware of this happening. I was in my cruiser on top of Beckjord Hill, as we used to call it, where there is absolutely nothing but deer playing. It was a safe place to wait for a radio run. Nothing.

I was totally left alone until Brian pulled up next to me with his son in his car and said, "How are you doing? Here's a drink. Do you need anything?" How he found me, I don't know to this day. Pierce Township is not an easy place to find someone if they don't want to be found. I was happy to see him. He understood how I felt.

After I was told the demonstrators left, I went back to the police station. The trustees were all there waiting for me, patting me on the back and saying, "It'll be okay. It'll be okay." But it wasn't okay, and I knew it never would be again as long as I was a police officer.

At home, talking to my wife, I said "Listen, I need to get out of there."

I was still seeing Doctor Daum and another police psychologist. Officers have to see the psychologist before they are allowed to return to work after a critical incident, so I had been seeing them for two years. I told Dr. Daum how I was feeling. He told me I needed to leave police work.

I said, "I can't." I didn't want to quit my job because of "them." I didn't want to let them have any satisfaction.

He said, "Well, being your doctor, I don't think it's healthy for you being in this job anymore. I'm going to have to make a recommendation to Chief Smith that you're done."

I asked him not to. I said, "Let me see if I can work through this." He let me go back to work.

The next few months went ok. Then on the first of the year, I got dispatched to a domestic violence call. It was a man I had arrested before. He had a warrant for domestic violence as well as the situation he was currently involved in. When the officer I was training that day and I got there the suspect was lying on the bed. I said, "C'mon, David, let's go to jail. Let's make this easy."

He says, "You're going to have to shoot me."

I said, "David, I'm not going to shoot you. Let's go."

"Shoot me!" he yelled back. Then he started cussing and screaming, demanding that I shoot him. I got on my radio to call in backup. I was saying to myself, "If he wants a fight, fine. But if I'm going to have to fight him, I'm going to have 25 of my closest buddies for backup and we will send him to jail."

He was still shouting, "Shoot me! You're going to have to shoot me!" while I was on the radio, so I didn't have to say much. The dispatcher could hear him yelling.

I quietly said, "Can you send me another car?"

Eddie Dye was the first one there. As he walked in the door, the suspect was still saying, "Shoot me." For ten minutes, that's all he said.

I looked at Eddie and tapped on my nightstick. He pulled his nightstick out and I readied my chemical irritant. I figured, "I'll spray him, and we'll take him out to jail, and all will be good with the world." So I kept talking to him, and I finally thought I got him to agree to go quietly.

But while I was cuffing him, his wife, who had been sitting in another room, blurted, "Just go to jail." He tried to push past me to get her, so I grabbed his hand and sprayed him with mace. The fight was on. We got him down on the ground pretty quickly. I hit him three times; twice for compliance and the third time to get him to drop a piece of glass he had grabbed.

We managed to subdue him, handcuff him and get him into the cruiser. We called the chief to let him know that we had a use of force and an injured prisoner.

After checking if everyone was alright, Chief Smith said, "I'll meet you at the hospital."

When I hung up the phone, I looked at my police car. The suspect had vanished even with an officer standing guard. My heart felt like one of those cartoon hearts that jump right out of your chest. I went over to my cruiser to confirm my suspicions and he was still there, laying across the back seat in the same position that Roger Owensby had been. I froze.

Eddie opened the door and tapped the man on the shoulder and said, "Dave, sit up straight." And he sat up straight. He had been lying down because he was hung over from the night before.

It scared the daylights out of me.

When we got to the hospital, the first thing our suspect tells my boss is "He choked me."

Chief Smith looked at him and asked, "Are you sure?"

He replied, "He choked me."

Hearing that, I could not breathe. My heart was hammering. I walked out of the emergency room ready to give up my badge and gun right then and there.

The chief caught up with me. He asked, "Are you all right?"

I said, "No, I'm not all right. I didn't touch him. I did not put a hand on him other than when I hit him three times like I told you before." I was so frustrated.

He said, "Yes, I know. I know he's lying."

I said, "Are you sure?" In the past, my bosses agreed with me in person and used me to their advantage in public. So I asked again, "Are you sure you know he's lying?"

Chief said, "I know he's lying. I know you wouldn't do that." Then he told me to go back to the office. I left.

Back at the station, I was still shaking. In fact, I was getting extremely nervous. I called my wife and said, "I don't know if I can keep doing this." She told me I needed to call Dr. Daum. When I spoke with Dr. Daum, I said, "I may be done. I just can't keep doing this."

And he said, "Talk to me on Monday and we will set something up."

The next day, June 29th, I backed up a state trooper on a traffic stop. Before the trial I used to be a proactive police officer. The minute someone started to get mouthy, the minute someone started to get a little physical, I would be the first one to step up. I wanted to keep things from escalating. I wanted to keep people from getting hurt. That day I realized I wasn't that cop anymore. I was afraid.

The trooper was giving someone a speeding ticket. No big deal. I was just there to back him up. But the driver started yelling at the trooper. Instead of taking a step forward, I started backing up. I was no longer confident in my ability to handle the job.

The next day, I couldn't even get into my police car. I stood there and looked at the door, but I couldn't make myself get in. I knew it was over. I could not hide my sadness when I called Chief Smith. "I'm done. I quit." I told him. He tried to talk me out of it, but I said, "I'm done. It's over. I can't even get in the patrol car." The chief told me to take the day off and sleep on it. I cried when I talked with him. To tell Chief Smith, who I admire so much, over the phone that I couldn't take it anymore was so humiliating. I was destroyed.

I didn't have a key to his office so I found two senior officers and I put my badge and gun belt on Vic's desk. The looks on their faces were of absolute disbelief as I walked out of the police department. I don't remember the drive home. I don't think I remember anything about the next week.

I couldn't stop crying as I told Kristen what happened that morning. She talked about a day a few months earlier when I told her I had to quit. She told me then to stick it out because she knew how much I loved police work and that I might eventually regret leaving. It wasn't like that this time. When I got home neither of us questioned my decision. We just sat with each other and cried.

I lost so much weight over that period of time because I was constantly worried. I was paranoid. I just couldn't live with that. It wasn't just that traffic stop. It was the totality of the circumstances.

I used to teach people at the academy when to be proactive, when to pull their gun out of their holster, when to do this, when to do that. But I also taught a class on when it's time to quit the job. All the signs were there in my case. I was having nightmares. I wasn't sleeping. I wasn't eating. I had no confidence. I didn't feel safe anymore. So the necessary paperwork was filed and in two months I would be retired.

My friendship with Chief Smith is one of the most important things that came out of this. The chief was very observant. When he saw that I was having a bad day we had "meetings". I could knock on his door and say, "Boss, can I talk to you for a minute?"

"Come on in Blaine. Shut the door behind you." He would say.

I'd sit in his office and talk about my feelings or what was going through my mind. He would listen and give me his clear advise whenever I needed it. He was a tremendous help to me when matters pertaining to my criminal or civil trials came up, even after I left Pierce Township.

If I had started my police career at Pierce Township instead of Cincinnati, I'd still be an officer there. Pierce was the ideal place for me to be. And when I retired, Pierce Township kept me on the payroll until my retirement benefits came through. That told me how they felt about me. Their words of trust and belief in me were manifested there. It wasn't just lip service.

After I left Pierce Township, Chief Smith instituted that canine patrol we had talked about. The officer they hired to replace me took that position. It always struck me as a warm kind of funny.

The news media didn't find out I quit until October, when something completely unrelated happened; a death in which a father shook a baby. One of the reporters said, "Where's Officer Jorg? I thought he was working day shift."

Chief says, "Okay, he quit back in June."

"Why did he leave?", "Where did he go?", "What is he doing now?", questioned the reporters.

Of course the chief "was not about to help them write a bad story about one of his officers" so they eventually left that subject alone. God bless Chief Smith.

Chapter 16
Firing Back

From the get-go, my dad insisted that I make people pay for the wrong they did to me. I resisted that opinion for the longest time. After a while, when I realized there would be no apology, my bitterness got the best of me and I decided that yes, people were going to have to answer for their deeds. We filed a civil suit against parties in the city and the county in federal court.

Most people I knew told me that I was found not guilty and to just let it go. They were growing weak with the weight of the turmoil just as I was. But, it was more than guilt or innocence in my eyes. My life and my person were permanently damaged. I didn't think anyone understood.

After hiring Bill Gustavson, a well known and respected Cincinnati attorney, we decided to file three lawsuits. In May, 2002, we filed a $30 million lawsuit against the City of Cincinnati, Hamilton County, and coroner Carl Parrott, Jr. M.D. in his official capacity only.

We sought to prove that the city officials wanted me charged with a crime because of mounting pressure from African-Americans who were unhappy with the conduct of the police. All the events surrounding the Owensby incident made me believe the powers that be needed a diversion to keep themselves out of the critical spotlight. Our suit contended: "The defendants... engaged in a course of conduct based on racial motives, and consequent political considerations, to find a white police officer a scapegoat."

We wanted to include Prosecutor Mike Allen as a defendant, but Ohio law guarantees prosecutorial immunity for anyone in his position. It seemed the most unscrupulous of them all was the one person I couldn't legally touch. Allen took an oath to uphold the law and find the truth. In my case, he did neither. He knew the truth, and chose to bury it. I was taught that truth provides direction. Allen and his staff knowingly elected to go down the wrong path. The investigation was not objective, and I suffered.

Allen knew from the beginning that there was no case against me. His staff told him he didn't have sufficient evidence to empanel a grand jury. But that didn't matter. Mr. Allen knew he could guide the grand jury to get his desired result. And he did. He did so knowing that, as prosecutor, he was immune from being held liable for the damage done by a wrongful charge. The Civil Rights Act of 1871 states that a prosecutor is, "absolutely immune from suit for malicious prosecution... " That immunity leaves genuinely wronged criminal defendants--like me--without civil redress.

Dr. Parrott, I thought, was another matter. He was wrong when he concluded that Owensby died from mechanical asphyxiation, which means he was deprived of oxygen by something outside his body. I think Dr. Parrott realized that he was wrong within days of making his conclusion. He could not prove a chokehold. There were no marks to the neck, internally or externally. And the petechia he found in just one eye could result from many things.

On November 19, 2000, just twelve days after Roger Owensby Jr. died, Dr. Parrott stated, "Until the investigation is complete, it will be impossible to know for certain how Mr. Owensby died. It gets real complicated, we've got a tangle of events here." That disagreed with his earlier statement that contributed to the rioting Cincinnati endured.

The court disagreed with our contention that Dr. Parrott was a policy maker for the county, and dismissed him from the lawsuit. I still feel that he should be held liable for his conduct. He had jurisdiction over the Owensby investigation. He labeled me the cause of death in the eyes of the public.

Now the county was the only defendant, which was strange because my only allegations against Hamilton County were based on Dr. Parrott's conduct. When the county's attorneys figured that out, they promptly filed a motion arguing that the county could not remain a defendant if the coroner was dismissed from the suit. They were right.

I was hopeful when the judge directed the case to mediation. At a mediation conference on September 23, 2004, the mediator asked me, "What do you want out of this case?"

My reply: "An apology from the city and county." No money, I just wanted an apology. The mediator took my request to the County, which declined it. The court said we could proceed on claims for malicious prosecution and false arrest against the city. Then the court reversed its decision and dismissed the malicious prosecution and the false arrest claims against the city. Our lawsuit was dead.

I couldn't believe it. The court completely left the County off the hook without giving us the opportunity to find what really happened. I was stunned that the court wouldn't give us a chance to engage in discovery to find out everything that went on behind the scenes.

In July 2002, Mr. Gustavson filed a defamation of character lawsuit against Rev. Damon Lynch III, the outspoken leader of the Cincinnati Black United Front (CBUF). The crux of the $10 million lawsuit was inflammatory and untrue statements Lynch had distributed on his organization's letterhead. The letter said, "Police are killing, raping, planting false evidence." Lynch also accused me of using, "marine-style choke hold to kill an unarmed Roger Owensby, Jr." Clearly, Lynch and the Black United Front had defamed me.

Mr. Gustavson spoke plainly, telling the Enquirer and WLW listeners, "If you're going to accuse Cincinnati Police officers of being murderers, if you're going to accuse Cincinnati Police officers of being rapists, and you're going to say that a Cincinnati Police officer used a Marine-style chokehold to kill somebody, you better be able to prove it."

Judge Robert Ruehlman threw the case out. Judge Ruehlman ruled that Lynch had merely offered an "opinion" when he accused me of killing Roger Owensby Jr. with a "marine-style chokehold." "The allegedly defamatory statements are the type of hyperbole and invective that public officers must simply endure..." Ruehlman wrote in his opinion. Of course, I didn't agree with the decision. I didn't see how a letter distributed on an organization's letterhead by a well known political activist to guide a mass of people to a particular action could be called just an "opinion". That key word protected Lynch's statements under the Fourth Amendment's freedom of speech.

There were some interesting moments at the hearing when we appealed. One judge inquired if I was a Marine. The answer was, "no." In fact, I've never been in the military. The attorney representing Rev. Lynch kept waiving a stack of newspaper articles in front of the three-judge panel, but nowhere did the papers state that evidence had been planted, anyone raped, or innocent civilians killed.

My appeal was denied on the grounds that the statement about planting evidence, raping and killing didn't mention me individually. But were, "general statements impugning the police." As for the statement that I killed Roger Owensby, Jr., the justices agreed with Judge Ruehlman that Lynch had been expressing an opinion, not fact. The appeals court ruled, "Based upon the totality of the circumstances we are convinced that the ordinary reader would accept CBUF's and Lynch's statements in their letter as opinions and not as facts. Therefore, under Ohio Constitution, the statements were protected speech." However, Mr. Lynch distributed that letter to convince the people it was truth. And how they should act on that truth.

Nearly six years after the death of Roger Owensby, I still feel like the courts let us down. I was especially bitter that the Federal lawsuit against the city and county was dismissed, because I know a great deal of information would have come out if my attorney could have gotten to the discovery phase. Mr. Gustavson and I both knew that people conspired against me, we just needed an opportunity to prove it. Gustavson kept saying, "We know there's something going on, but we haven't been able to depose anybody."

He was right. Something had gone on. One such something was brought to our attention by an honest Cincinnati officer with first hand knowledge. The city had persuaded Dr. Wecht, the medical expert they hired to support their coroners, Dr. Parrott and Dr. Schultz, to be less than truthful about how Roger Owensby, Jr. died.

Pat called me with the news. He got the information from Don Hardin. Mr. Hardin was the FOP attorney representing the police officers in the civil suit the Owensby estate brought against the City of Cincinnati, et. al. Hardin was contacted by a high-ranking Cincinnati Police official who was privy to the reports Dr. Wecht wrote. There were "reports". Plural.

Dr. Wecht issued his findings on the original autopsy on August 8, 2002. On August 14, five city officials quietly flew to Pittsburgh to meet with Dr. Wecht. After that visit, Dr. Wecht revised his report and gave the city a second version on September 10, 2002.

My private civil attorney, Bill Gustavson, tried to answer some big questions during a November 15, 2004 telephone deposition. Dr. Wecht admitted there were two reports, and that he reviewed both of them, but said, "I don't know why two reports were issued."

According to Dr. Wecht, the only difference between the two reports was on page one, where the name "Hunter" was added. "Otherwise, they are exactly the same," Dr. Wecht insisted. Later, he remarked, "The fact that a report has been submitted on August 8 and another report was generated does give me pause. I left the report open, and yet a (second) report had been submitted. So, you know, I don't know what that means."

What it means is that either Dr. Wecht was lying, or someone altered his report substantially. The original version is fourteen pages. The September 10 report is seventen pages.

Dr. Wecht may have been manipulated by the city, but he never did find anything they needed to hang me. Dr. Wecht stated that a "...combination (of factors) is very likely." He specifically mentioned "heart occlusion." The medical dictionary I consulted says the following: "occlude", which means, "To close, obstruct, or prevent the passage. To occlude an artery is to occlude the flow of blood."

Dr. Wecht also mentioned that mace and an arm over nose/mouth could be contributing factors but they were not provable. Dr. Wecht concluded by saying, "I leave the report open."

Dr. Wecht also didn't seem to have all of the evidence when he made his report. When a TV reporter mentioned that six witnesses saw Owensby walk to the police car. Dr. Wecht responded, "What do you mean they have six witnesses who saw him walk to the car?"

The facts surrounding Dr. Wecht's differing reports were a clear indicator that there was more evidence to be found. It was the first concrete piece of evidence we had. I wondered what other incriminating information would we have discovered if we had been able to depose people?

The official who revealed Dr. Wecht's rewritten reports was in the process of retiring. I understand that he was very upset and disgusted with how the City of Cincinnati handled these things. He came to Don Hardin. He said "This is wrong" and he laid all the evidence out on the table.

The following pages are from the forensics expert that my attorney asked to review to cause of death of Roger Owensby Jr:

AFFIDAVIT

The undersigned, being duly cautioned and sworn, deposes and states as follows:

1.   My name is Charles V. Wetli, M.D. I am a physician and the Chief Medical Examiner of Suffolk County, located at Hauppauge, New York. I am also a Clinical Professor of Pathology at the State University of New York at Stony Brook, New York. I have been board certified in Anatomic and Clinical Pathology since 1974, and in Forensic Pathology since 1979. Attached is a true and accurate copy of my Curriculum Vitae, updated as of July 3, 2002.

2.   I have personally performed nearly 7000 autopsies and have supervised and reviewed thousands more. Numerous cases involved the evaluation of asphyxia, strangulation and choke holds.

3.   I was consulted by the attorney for R. Blaine Jorg to review the autopsy of Roger Owensby, Jr., to determine the cause of death of Mr. Owensby. I have reviewed the autopsy report of Roger Owensby, Jr., the microscopic slides from the autopsy, the autopsy photographs, the University Hospital medical report, the EMS record, various photographs, including photographs of Ariel St. Clair and George Weaver with their arms around the neck of a police officer, the property report of the evidence recovered concerning Mr. Owensby, the trial testimony of Dr. Daniel L. Schultz, who performed the autopsy of Roger Owensby, Jr., and statements of witnesses Brian Menefee, Ariel St. Clair, George Weaver, and Police Officer Robert Heiland. Although other evidentiary materials are available, I am able to render an opinion on the cause of death of Roger Owensby, Jr., based on the above described items, all of which are hereby incorporated by reference. All of the opinions that I describe in this affidavit are based on my personal knowledge, my review of the evidentiary materials described above, based on my education, training and experience, and I hold all of my opinions to a reasonable degree of medical certainty.

4.   Roger Owensby, Jr., did not die from any type of asphyxia, including a mechanical asphyxia, or a choke hold. Roger Owensby, Jr., died a sudden cardiac death - i.e. an

148

(adrenaline) and nor-epinephrine. Further, it has been shown that many such individuals also experience profound metabolic acidosis, which may also lead to a sudden cessation of cardiac function.

5.   The following are the basis for my opinion that Roger Owensby, Jr., died from Sudden Cardiac Death:

- The death occurred suddenly;
- There is a chest wall injury, but no evidence that there was chest compression with no ability to breath for 3-5 minutes, which would be necessary to cause an asphyxia;
- There is absolutely no evidence of neck injury;
- It is inconceivable that a forearm bar hold as demonstrated in the photographs of St. Clair and/or Weaver would not leave any injury in the neck of a non-sedated, struggling man with the habitus of Mr. Owensby;
- Sudden loss of vital signs after an intense period of physical exertion is typical for a cardiac arrhythmia;
- Additionally, the petechiae, which are pinpoint hemorrhages in the white portion of the eye, are not adequately depicted in the autopsy photographs, casting doubt on their actual existence;
- However, if you assume that there were petechiae in the right eye, but not depicted in the photograph of the left eye, as testified to by Dr. Schultz, it would be evidence of a localized injury to the right eye like you would receive from an irritant or dirt, not from an asphyxia. If Mr. Owensby had been asphyxiated, there would have been bilateral petechiae, or equal petechiae in both eyes, which would have been easily observed and photographed;
- The bruises to Mr. Owensby's back are consistent with blows from a fist, not from compression with knees as testified to by Dr. Schultz; and

– Witnesses indicated Mr. Owensby walked from the arrest scene to the police car, and then had a sudden loss of vital signs while alone in the police car, which means that Roger Owensby, Jr., could not have died during his arrest, but died from a sudden cardiac event in the police car.

FURTHER AFFIANT SAYETH NAUGHT.

_____
Charles V. Wetli, M.D.

Personally appearing before me this 13th day of September, 2002, was Charles V. Wetli, M.D., known to me, who swore that the foregoing was true to the best of his knowledge and belief.

Vera Moras
Notary Public, State of New York
No. 4893719
Qualified in Suffolk County
Commission Expires May 18, 2003

_____
Notary Public

CERTIFICATE OF SERVICE

This is to certify that a copy of this motion has been served on all counsel of record on this ___ day of September, 2002, by regular U.S. mail, postage prepaid.

_____
William M. Gustavson

150

Chapter 17
The Black Hole

My descent into what I call, "the black hole" probably started one day when I left the office of my attorney, Scott Croswell, after he told me, "Blaine, they don't have a choice. They're going to indict you. There is going to be a grand jury called."

At the time, I was unsure about Croswell. It was very confusing. Pat and I had spent a lot of time going over things with Don Hardin, the FOP-appointed attorney. No matter how we looked at the case in Hardin's office, the prosecutor's office didn't have anything. Yet, Croswell was telling me I was going to be indicted.

My wife, Kristen, trusted Croswell, and that counted for a lot. She thought he was trying to be as straight as possible with me. Each time something new happened in my case, it was a big surprise to me. She thought he was trying to keep me level while the unbelievable happened. But she wasn't the one in the spotlight, I was.

Really, all of us were in denial. Everyone I knew was telling me, "There is no case. There's nothing they can do to you. You're going to get your job back. You're going to get your badge back." We all believed the legal process would work honestly.

It was definitely a slow descent into the black hole, but once it began, I couldn't see any way to climb out of my personal abyss. I remember the day I was arrested. It was so surreal sitting in the back chamber of the judge's office and having him slide the paperwork in front of me. I helped him fill out the paperwork for my own arrest. When I left the jail that night, I needed a release. A few of my friends came over and we toasted to our distaste of the current city government.

The next day, I was sitting in the basement, still in shock, and I remember the Discovery Channel was showing, "The World's Toughest Prisons." I couldn't tear myself away. I started watching TV shows about prisons; Alcatraz, Leavenworth, Sing Sing, all of the big ones. I began thinking about how my case could go terribly wrong, which led me to brush up on my

Me, Goofy and Kristen at Disney World, June 2001

self-defense. I was thinking, If I have to go to prison, I'm going to have to fight. Everyday. Because if you're a police officer who's been sent to prison, there are only two things that could happen: I get killed, or I teach them what I know so they could use it on the streets against cops. Not in favor of either, I planned how I could get put into solitary confinement as soon as I got to prison.

No one could reach me when I was in the black hole. I stopped talking to Kristen. I wouldn't respond when she asked me questions. When she asked what I was thinking about, my answer was always the same, "Nothing." I just sat in front of the TV all day.

I didn't want to go anywhere, not even to church. I didn't want to confront it anymore. Everyone kept telling me, it's going to be okay. Everyone kept consoling me, which only made me angry. I thought, "How in the heck do you know?"

I turned my back on God, and my faith. I turned my back on my family. I turned my back on my wife. The only one I didn't turn my back on was Pat. He and I were in similar situations. He and I were partners in the police world. He was the only one I could talk to.

My trial kept getting moved back. Every time there was a postponement, it was like someone was twisting a knife in my back. The date originally set in the spring turned into June 24. Croswell told me, "It's going. It's a firm date. They'll have jury selection."

My sister called me from California and told me that she was going to take everyone to Disney World to celebrate when the trial was over. That was a bright spark for me. I was looking forward to all of us being together when it was finally over. I needed to think about when it was over.

Then, five days before the trial, another postponement. The judge had to leave town on some pressing matter. That was a real let down. So my sister asked, do we still go to Florida when the trial won't happen until afterward? I just said, "Yeah, let's do it. It will be our pre-victory party." So we did. My three sisters and their families, my parents and Kristen and I went to Disney World. It was miserable. It was the happiest place on earth versus me. So many great things were going on and I didn't want to be there. My mind was still back at home on the trial.

One day, I didn't want to go to the park and Dad stayed at the hotel with me. We sat on the tailgate of my pick-up truck and had a heart-to-heart talk. I talked with Dad about my fears but, I got so angry that this was happening to me that I had to get up and leave.

Back home in Ohio, I was sleeping twelve to fourteen hours a day. I was trying to avoid the stress but, I was being consumed by it instead. Eventually, I ended up in the hospital. I had gall bladder surgery. The surgeon said stress was a contributing factor. Before I knew it the summer had flown by with no trial, then July, August, September, and October. All that time we were discovering fishy things about my case.

As the new trial date came closer, my depression was getting worse and worse. Later, Kristen told me that the look on my face through those months was scary. I was no longer the happy-go-lucky man she had married. I didn't know it at the time, but Kristen was afraid of me. She didn't know me, and she didn't know how to bring the Blaine she knew back.

Every night, I went to bed angry, dead to the world, even to those closest to me. I was seeing Dr. Daum, but I don't know how much the therapy was helping me. He only confirmed that what I was feeling was natural, given what I had gone through. I told him I thought I was turning into a racist, and he said, "That's perfectly natural. That's how people become racists. Something is done to them by a people of another race."

I remember thinking, "This guy is suposed to tell me how to get better. But instead, he's telling me that I should feel the way I do."

I had become jaded. The naive, cheerful guy who was always pleasant and upbeat, who never saw the bad in anybody, was gone. I had always lived by the ideal that if you do things to best of your ability, and were honest and followed all the rules, everything would be okay. But the opposite had happened. My understanding of the world was flip-flopped.

I continued to feel that way after my trial. I had been vindicated, and things seemed more positive for a short while. Then I was assigned to the Impound lot. That was degrading.

By then, I couldn't stand being around other officers. I hated everybody. Even Kristen. She tried to understand, but it was taking a toll on her. She knew what the problem was, but she couldn't reach me.

I didn't want to heal.

If I am accused long enough of doing something, I figure, I might as well do it. People kept accusing me of being this racial predator, this social monster. They convicted me before the trial even started. I heard about how terrible I was every day. Finally, I thought, "Then that's who they're going to get."

The "N" word was always a detestable word to me. When I was in seventh grade, I had the opportunity to try out for a select traveling football team and eighty percent of the guys trying out were black. I didn't care. Color never concerned me. I was the only kid in my neighborhood who had black friends. I'd stay at their house, and they'd stay at mine. What's the big deal?

Not long ago, I found the old roster of that team and five of our players lived in Bond Hill, at addresses where I had arrested people. But, the boys I knew were great guys.

When I was at Elder High School, there was one black student, Aaron. We were friends. One day I saw three guys giving Aaron a hard way to go so I stood in front of them and said that if they wanted a piece of Aaron, they'd have to go through me. It never dawned on me that they were picking on a black kid. I just thought they were picking on Aaron because he was smaller than them.

After the trial I became a racist. I hate to admit it, but I did promise to tell the truth in this book. I was full of anger, and I had nowhere to direct it. I embraced that "N" word and started using it with vigor.

About four and a half years after the incident my friend Ron and his family moved in with us. He had been diagnosed with post traumatic stress disorder as I had and had to leave police work, too. Eight people were living in our two-bedroom house, and two of them were retired cops with PTSD.

What I went through was bad, but what Ron went through was worse. He was the first officer on the scene when Officer Kevin Crayon got dragged to his death. He was first on the scene when Officers Pope and Jeter got killed. He was there when Alonzo Davenport, the man who shot Pope and Jeter, turned the gun on himself. Three days after that, Ron and his partner stopped a man on Vine Street, and the man grabbed Ron's gun. Every suspect he dealt with in those critical situations was black. So from that aspect,

Ron didn't help me. He was already damaged himself and was not ready to give black society any credit.

When it came to the nightmares and the daily flashbacks, Ron was a big help. He knew what I was going through, because he had them too. We were in my barn once when I had a flashback. Ron knew exactly what was happening. He helped me deal with them and didn't judge me because of them. It was just weird; two messed up cops who couldn't help themselves, trying to help each other.

I broke a lot of things when I was in the black hole. I threw things, and after a while Kristen made me promise that I would not break anything either of us really liked. That rule made me stop for a second when I was in a rage because I had to decide what was ok to break. That was the only bit of rationality I possessed at the time.

We found a diversion during that time. Both my wife and I are avid history lovers. We met some neighbors who were active in Civil War re-enacting and it sounded wonderful. Kristen and I went with them to lots of won-derful historical towns, dressed up in Civil War clothes, rode horses and pretended to be someone else. Even there Owensby followed me. One of the re-enactors recognized me and told me "you are only allowed to dress in blue. If anyone ever got a picture of you in a grey uniform you'll never live it down. After that, re-enacting wasn't much of an escape.

Kristen wanted me to get a job. When I left Cincinnati for Pierce Township I took a pay cut of about half my income. When I retired my income was cut in half again.

I tried to hold a job at the local feed store where I would be around local farmers that I liked. Two weeks into that job one of my co-workers recog-nized me and gave me the nickname "Nigger-slayer". I quit.

A few months later I tried working in the back room of a restaurant where not many people would see me. It wasn't long before I couldn't stand being around anyone at all. Once again, my job only lasted about two weeks.

Five years after that struggle in the parking lot with Roger Owensby, Jr. Kristen would find me sitting on the floor up against the wall in the corner of our bedroom. She told me when it was all over that she was afraid I was going to blow my brains out. I had thought about it. She didn't know what to do, so she went to Ron. He told her that she had to convince me to give up all my guns and ammunition. We lived in the country by now, so there were handguns and hunting guns in the house. I let them take all of them and Ron hid them. He didn't tell Kristen where he put them, just in case I tried to get it out of her later.

My wife was on suicide watch. If she didn't see me for a while, she would come looking for me. If I was in the barn too long, she'd check on me. Later, she told me that every time she came looking for me, she was afraid the she would find me with a bullet in my head or hanging from a rafter in the barn. She knew I didn't want to live.

The shrink wasn't helping me. I was seeing a counselor, a psychologist, a psychiatrist, and all they were giving me was medications and rationalizations for why its ok to feel this way. No one was telling me how to recover.

Chapter 18

State of Grace

I remember the Sunday morning after the incident. My wife and I went to church as usual. I remember people from our congregation coming up and talking to me. Giving their support, telling me that it will be ok. I sat through the service and felt very uncomfortable. I felt everyone was looking at me. I prayed for some reason or a meaning for all that was happening. I heard no response.

After returning to church and having the same process repeat itself, I became bitter and empty. I didn't want to go anymore. I hatched creative ways I could get us to miss the service. I would wake up in the middle of the night and turn off the alarm so we would over sleep. I would complain of a headache or some other ailment that would force me to stay home.

Over time I stopped looking for a reason for my ordeal and started to cast blame. I can't say that it helped, but I felt like I was at least doing something. After all I had been through, the loss of my faith affected me the most. I hated God, how could he do this to me? What did I do to deserve the treatment I was getting? I was always told that God answers prayers. Well He must have had me on hold because I never heard one!

In actuality I was getting the answers I asked for. God does answer prayers, but sometimes they are not the answers we want. He does say no to us, and that took me a long time to figure out.

When my wife and I moved to our farm, she would beg me to go to church, but then I had a built-in excuse. I had just gotten the job at Pierce Township. I was the only officer to work on Sundays so I couldn't go to church no matter how much she wanted me to. Things didn't change much when I left Pierce either. I hadn't been to church in so long, that it wasn't hard to perpetuate missing it.

I continued to meet with my doctors, and they were doing their best to treat me. All the medications that I was on were taking a toll on me. I hated the fact that I had to be medicated. The medication had its benefits, don't get me wrong. I could think rationally, and I wasn't always feeling down. On medication I felt I was starting to make some progress in leaving the incident behind, but at the same time I knew that something was missing.

That's when Kristen started giving me some really tough love. She told me that I had to get off the couch and get on with my life, that she can't keep living for the both of us. She said that if I really wanted to be better I would have started healing by now.

My first reaction was horrible resentment. I thought, "How dare you tell me how I am!" So I adopted the "I'll show you" plan. "I'll play by your rules, only better" I sneered inside myself. I did what she expected and more. I even went to church, but I hated it. I stood there every Sunday blankly waiting for the service to end. I wouldn't sing, and as soon as church was over I was out the door.

I called my buddy Jeff to see if I could get a little sympathy. His wife told me he was at their other farm a county away so I jumped in my truck and drove down to see him. When I got there he was in his fields on the tractor. I hopped up on his tractor and we rode around together for about three hours. I told Jeff that Kristen was getting on me about not being a husband. I was so angry, I almost yelled at him like I wanted to yell at Kristen. I told him everything I was feeling and waited for some sympathy. I didn't get it from Jeff. He prefaced his response by telling me that he loved me and Kristen and considered us to be family. He continued with his observations about my behavior and told me how I had been acting toward people lately. As you could imagine I didn't want to hear this from a friend, but I'm glad I did. His parting words of wisdom were to not just to go to church, but to be a part of the church and that I would start to see what I needed to get well.

Early on one Sunday morning, Kristen woke me up and said we were going to church. As I started to object, she said that if I didn't go with her she would go by herself. Even with her stern words I chose to stay behind and find something else to do. While she was gone I realized that she was trying to help me and I was mistreating her.

That next Saturday she asked if she would be going to church alone again. I wasn't sure how to respond. On Sunday morning she woke me up and said "lets go!" I went, but I was kicking and screaming inside the whole way there. Something happened that Sunday. I felt a peace that I had not felt in a long while. I could tell that Pastor felt personally every word he was telling us, and it almost seemed that he was talking straight to me.

When the service was over, I waited until almost the entire congregation was gone before I made my way to Pastor. I approached him and I asked him if he had a minute. He took me to his office where I asked him if I could talk to him for a while. Pastor preaches at two churches and had to leave for the second service so, we made an appointment for the next Tuesday.

When I showed up on that Tuesday, I explained to him my situation, my fears, and my feeling about God. How my faith was tarnished, and that I was in serious doubt. I told him I no longer thought God was listening to me and that I thought it was too late for me to ever be able to hear Him again. As Pastor listened to me I could see the intense look on his face grow. When I was finished, he said that he wasn't going to respond to my thoughts at that point, instead he wanted me to read the book of Job and he would meet with me again next Tuesday.

On Sunday he asked me how my reading assignment was going, and I told him that I finished Job.

He said "great, read the book of John also." At first I thought he was kidding, but he assured me he wasn't. At our Tuesday meeting, we discussed Job and John, we talked for about an hour and a half.

When I started to talk about me again he told me to read another book, this time the book of Romans. Man! All I wanted was some answers, and it seemed all I got was reading assignments.

I took his instructions anyway and read the next book.

When we met again, it was the same scenario. We discussed the books, and I questioned him about what they meant to me. He answered me by quoting what it was that I had read. It started to become clear to me that Pastor was a wise man. He didn't use his own words to tell me what I needed to hear.

All those prayers I have been praying over the past few years had been answered. The answers were right in front of me. Pastor opened my eyes. He talked about my life before all the controversy. He talked about the time since. Suddenly, I could see how God got me through my darkest hours. God gave me those dark hours as a gift to teach me. Without those hard days I could not be the person He wanted me to become. And there was a purpose. He wanted something of me.

...also rejoice in your sufferings, because we know that suffering produces perseverance; perseverance character; and character, hope. And hope does not disappoint us, because God has poured out his love into our hearts by the Holy Spirit, whom He has given us.
ROMANS 5:4

I had been dead to the world for about five years. I didn't even try to live. After my first meeting with Pastor, Kristen told me that there was a spark of life in my eyes that she had not seen in years.

I was on a good road to recovery. My psychiatrist finally found a balance of medicines to help me handle the flashbacks and nightmares, I was finding ways to take out my physical frustration in a productive manor, and my spirit was encouraged. As I got more involved in the church, Pastor and I discussed my future, which seemed to be unstable. As we talked the question of being a pastor and sharing my story, and my restored faith was presented.

I thought "me, a pastor?"

He explained to me that most pastors aren't the people who wanted to do this all their lives. They are the ones who had something happen to them that opened their eyes to the power and glory of God. Just about everyone I know uses the phrase "everything happens for a reason." The problem is, we as people want to know the reasons now! But God doesn't work like that. God is God, and He will do things the way He sees fit, and for us to try to reason His wisdom is unreasonable.

I didn't doubt anymore. I knew He was calling me. It was as if God was standing behind me telling me that He has gently nudged me, shoved me, then He had to hit me over the head with a cricket bat to get my attention.

I went home and told Kristen and immediately called the seminary to find out how to make it happen.

That was the spring of 2005, it is now the fall of 2006, and I have been studying to be a pastor for three terms now. Our church has named me the youth group leader while I am in seminary. Because of God and His infinite wisdom I embrace what happened to me. He has given me a new and more powerful passion.

God surely moves in mysterious ways. I have found out that no matter what has gone on in the past several years, He has given me my true calling. I remember seeing a news report after the civil suits where decided. Mr. Owensby, Sr. said that he has found some peace and that he hopes all the officers find some as well. I have peace. I had it all along in the truth and facts of the case, and never knew it, but most importantly I have peace in the grace and mercy that my Lord and Savior has given me.

God never said life would be easy. But as a loving Father He gives us "chores" as lessons to grow our character. To teach us to be like Him and to learn how to love in all circumstances.

This July at a youth leader's conference, Reverend Bill Yonker told a story. Since the day I heard it, it has affected me deeply. It has helped me minister to many people:

While on his way to Iowa for a conference, Reverend Yonker met a rather cartoonish young man at the airport. He asked if the Reverend was the youth minister he was supposed to pick up. They gathered up the luggage and proceeded to the young man's vehicle. His van was a work in progress to say the least, no radio and only one seat for the driver. As Pastor Yonker sat on the floor of the van looking up at this nineteen year-old kid, who looks like Shaggy from Scooby doo mixed with a little bit of a surfer dude, Pastor Yonker noticed a plastic spoon hanging around the neck on a chain of the young man. Pastor Yonker asked what the young man has been doing in his ministry at his age. The kid told him that he is part of an outreach program at his church, and he travels a bit. The kid told of the last time he went to Chicago with his ministry partner to minister in the red light district and gay bars. Pastor Yonker was intrigued to say the least, "Shaggy" continued to tell him that he and his partner entered the bar and stood around for a while until a seat at the bar opened up. As they sat observing the crowd, the young man asked a twenty something young man next to him if he came here often.

His response was, "I'm not working tonight, leave me alone."

"Shaggy" slowly worked into a conversation where he was able to ask how this twenty something got into prostitution. The man replied that he went to Chicago after high school to try acting. However it was a slow and painful process and he ended up selling himself just to eat. As "shaggy" listened, he asked if the young man would like to pray for help and guidance. The man responded, "no, but you can pray for me."

"Ok, tonight when I get to my hotel I will pray for you." Shaggy said.

"Would you pray for me now, right here?' the young man asked.

So in the middle of this club the two of them prayed for forgiveness, and understanding. When they concluded their prayer, "shaggy" asked how long it has been since the young man has called his parents. He responded with, "too long". The young man said that when his parents found out about his life style years ago, they did not approve and their relationship was nonexistent. "shaggy" convinced the man to step out side and call his parents. After a ten minute conversation, there were tears in the man's eyes, as he handed the phone to "shaggy".

'I'm going home to see my folks." He told "shaggy". "they can't wait to see me!"

As Pastor Yonker heard the conclusion of this he realized he was now the student of this nineteen year-old. There was a brief silence until Pastor Yonker asked what the spoon was for. The response he got still makes me think.

"Shaggy" said, "if you look in your silverware drawer, you will notice that knives are for cutting, forks are for stabbing, but spoons are to serve. I can't tell you how many people I have cut, and stabbed with harsh words and unkind actions. This plastic spoon is to remind me that I am a servant."

Sometimes I wish this whole ordeal had never happened, but that would be a mistake. It's a gift.

I only hope that the reader of this book comes away with an understanding of a few things.

First, the police are doing a very dangerous job. The support they get from their communities, family, superiors, and governing bodies is vital to their ability to handle the daily stresses.

Second, the vast majority of police officers do their job right every day, day-in and day-out.

Third, until you see what an officer has to do on a daily basis, never prejudge him or her.

Most importantly, that God is love, and God is good. Eventually man will fail you but, God never will.

I would like to remind everyone that policing is not a black/white issue, or brown, green or whatever, it is about one thing: right and wrong. If we all remember to do what is right, not wrong, do what is good, not bad, and to stand up in the face of adversity, we will be justly judged by our Maker. Men may treat you unjustly but when you can bear the weight no longer, God will bear it for you.

> When Jesus spoke again to the people, he said, "I am the light of the world. Whoever follows me will never walk in darkness, but will have the light of life."
> John 8:12

God Bless... Be spoons

Epilogue

After my deposition in the Owensby civil suit, Mike Allen told the press that I was pathetic "a liar and bitter." I have no hatred for Mr. Allen. He might have tried to ruin my life but in the end he didn't succeed. Am I bitter? I used to be. But am I a liar? I have held to the truth from day one. A liar tells a man's father in private "if your son isn't convicted I won't lose any sleep over it", and then rails on that same man publicly.

There is a wide gap between what is labeled legal fact and what is actual truth. Upon finding out that I was writing this book, two interesting things happened. The Owensby family's attorney sent a letter to the individual helping me put this book together, telling him to make sure that the book was consistent with what was upheld by the courts. When a response to that letter was sent, detailing the flaws in their "admissible evidence", we never heard from them again. Then, the Owensby family settled out of court for $6,500,000. When my attorney sent me the final papers from that suit, I had reservations about signing them. I wanted the civil case to go to court. I wanted justice. But what I wanted most was to get on with my life.

During preparation for the civil suit, my FOP attorney Don Hardin contacted several well known use of force experts. All of them had the opportunity to review the evidence available and all of them reported that the officers' actions and behavior that night were either, "sound judgment", "within policy and procedure" or "legally, morally, and ethically correct". They pointed out why any good cop in this situation would have no reason to believe that the suspect was in any mortal danger and that once secured in another officer's car, my responsibility, along with the officers in the struggle, was over.

This entire event has had a great toll on me, my fellow officers, the Owensby family, and the city. It is a shame that politics has that kind of power. We as a people need to learn from this event and the events surrounding us to see where our community is heading. We have too many people in authority that are in denial about the violence that is taking advantage of this city. The violence is getting worse, families are being destroyed, and no one seems to care.

Some people want the police to be nice, touchy feely and gentile. But there is no nice way to arrest some one who doesn't want to be arrested. There are many tools at the disposal for police officers these days. Sometimes it seems to be too many. I have heard the posturing of the police chief on the news, and the spin of statistics by the politicians. I have also heard the outcry for help by the community that wants to be able to let their kids go outside and play with out the fear of someone's gunfire.

Until people start to support their police and work together to get the evil-doers off the street, there will be no hope. People will continue to move out of the city in record numbers. I know that the city's police force is willing and able to do the job that is needed. And they will succeed when the community realizes that the cops are not the bad guys. The police are the ones willing to lay their life on the line for you.

As for me, I will continue through seminary, and work on my farm. There is a saying, "If God brings you to it, He will get you through it." He brought me through this horrible half decade and now He has given me peace. I no longer feel the weight of hatred. I no longer fear the threats. I am free.

To contact the author go to:
www.13minutes.org

HELMER, MARTINS, RICE & POPHAM
CO., L.P.A.

ATTORNEYS AT LAW

Fourth & Walnut Centre, Suite 1900
105 East 4th Street
Cincinnati, Ohio 45202-4008

...es B. Helmer, Jr.*
...l B. Martins
...e Webster Popham**
...ert M. Rice
...ald G. Stiens, Jr.
...nifer L. Lambert
...l M. Schenz
D.C. Bar
...o KY Bar

Telephone: (513) ▮▮▮▮▮
Telecopier: (513) ▮▮▮▮

Of Counsel:
Robert Clark Neff, Jr.

February 23, 2006

VIA CERTIFIED MAIL
RETURN RECEIPT REQUESTED

Re: *Robert Blaine Jorg*

Dear Mr. ▮▮▮▮

    I read with interest the article at NPDF.net concerning Robert Blaine Jorg which reports that you are planning to publish a book entitled "Thirteen Minutes: The Factual Story of the Owensby Case and Of the Cops Involved in the Arrest." Based on the numerous false statements of fact contained in the National Police Defense Foundation webpage article, I enclose for your information the true facts surrounding the death of Roger Owensby, Jr., as found by the United States District Court for the Southern District of Ohio based upon admissible evidence and sworn testimony. The enclosed United States District Court decision finds that the police officers as well as the City of Cincinnati and its Chief of Police were liable for the violation of Mr. Owensby's constitutional right to medical care.

    Further, I enclose the decision of the United States Court of Appeals for the Sixth Circuit affirming the trial court's the denial of qualified immunity to the Cincinnati police officers based upon their conduct on the evening of November 7, 2000.

    You now have before you the actual facts. Please ensure that any publication authored by you comports with these facts.

Sincerely,

Paul B. Martins

PBM:kmr
Enclosures
cc: AuthorHouse TM (Certified Mail w/enclosures)

167